Success has a name
Jesus Christ!

Tamara Demontis

Title book: **Success has a name - Jesus Christ!**

Author book: Tamara Demontis

© 2024, Tamara Demontis
Publisher: BoD • Books on Demand GmbH, In de Tarpen 42, 22848 Norderstedt
Printed by: Libri Plureos GmbH, Friedensallee 273, 22763 Hamburg
ISBN: 978-3-7597-9545-8

Introduction

A note from the Author;
The following Story is based on true events.

Business and spirituality have always been seen as opposites, but is this really true?

In spirituality, people can reconnect with their deepest resources to face change with new energy and effectively deal with challenges and complexity. Developing intimacy with one's own intuition and training oneself to recognise its sources, understanding oneself as part of a larger system and building a flowing bridge between rationality and spirituality are elements that make it possible to work on several levels at the same time and create the ideal conditions for real success. Success is understood as a form of personal development through work and, in absolute terms, through one's own life choices, thanks to the ability to understand oneself in its various dimensions and integrate them into daily life in a balanced way.

There is no true wealth if our minds do not know how to control it and how to live it. And there is no true inner happiness if one is excluded from the circle of material wealth. We have a purpose in life, a unique gift or a special talent to use for ourselves and others.

And when we put our talents and ourselves at the service of others, we experience the ecstasy and exultation of the spirit, which is the highest purpose of our existence. Discovering what we can do better than anyone else in the world means discovering our own talent. To do this, we must concentrate on what we can offer to others by being useful to humanity. Then, we should rediscover our divinity and our true talent and use them to help others. In this way, we would all create the wealth we desire, knowing that we are spiritual beings with material experience and not material beings with physical experience.

This book is for all people whose hearts cry out for success, regardless of whether they are men or women, their social class and religion, and where in the world they are. Begin, for the way shows itself as you go!

Table of Contents

Chapter 1 The road to success

"Jesus, where are you? Why hast thou forsaken me?" sobbed Viktoria, frightened by the sound of gunfire as she knelt in the half-light in front of her bed.

"Jesus, do you hear me?" she said softly.

"Jeesuuus!!!" she screamed angrily with all the air in her lungs.

Suddenly, she heard a soft knock at the window and started to tremble. She quickly hid under the bed while the soft knocking at the window continued. Terrified and curious simultaneously, she looked at the window and recognised the shadow.

"How did you get here?" she asked with tears in her eyes.

It was 1991 when Croatia declared itself an independent state, and the Yugoslav People's Army started the war. Terrified, Viktoria ran away at night and left her beloved country at age 21 to come to Germany. Coming from a country that was not considered a developing country but with many visions of the future, she found herself overnight in a country whose development and industrialisation were not even remotely comparable to that of her native Croatia.

"Where have we landed?" she asked her husband Ivan at Mannheim's central railway station. Yes, her husband, because the 21-year-old Viktoria had only been married for two days when she arrived in Germany.

"What bothers you most here: the chaos, the language you don't understand, or the grey sky at the end of July?" he asked, amused, as she looked around.

But she did not know if anything bothered her; everything was different from what she was used to seeing in her country. The buildings, the many people from different cultures around her, and the trams running on the tracks in front of the station. She had never seen such means of transport before. She closed her eyes for a moment and looked at the unpaved roads of Croatia, where the car's shock absorbers screamed at every pothole and smiled to herself.

"Hey, are you listening to me?" her irritated husband asked.

"Come on, let's get on the tram and look at the flat," she replied, eager to see what would come next.

Tired from the long journey by car and train from Croatia to Mannheim but glad to be out of danger and far away from the war, she sat silently in the tram, gazing dreamily out while memories of when she was a 14-year-old girl filled her mind. She returned briefly to the past and sat with her friends in the middle of her parents' vineyard, euphorically talking about their visions of the future. She had drawn up her life plan at an early age, and her goals were few but clearly defined, at least as far as children and career were concerned, for she had already planned to have her first child at the age of 23 and to become a successful businesswoman.

But whenever she spoke of her great visions, her friends looked at her as if she were an alien and said: "Are you listening to yourself?

At 23, you will not even have finished your studies, let alone become a mother. How can you imagine becoming a successful businesswoman in Croatia? You know that our economy is based on agriculture, crafts, and tourism, and most women stay at home when they have a child. Make sure that you marry a wealthy boy from a good family."

But at 21, Viktoria was already married, and her young husband, Ivan, came from a good family but was not wealthy. Nevertheless, Ivan saved her life by taking her away from the war-torn country. From an early age, Viktoria recognised the narrow horizons of her friends, who, like her, came from humble families and lived by the motto 'better poor than good Christian'. With her big-picture way of thinking, she was something of the group's black sheep, and not just among her friends, for not even among her family could she talk about such visions without being ridiculed.

ViKtoria's family came from a modest background, and her parents were content with what they had, so they taught her and her siblings to do the same. This was the basis of her parents' upbringing, which saw money as bad or cursed. But while for some of her siblings, this upbringing in poverty was no problem, for her, it caused a real disgust, and she was reluctant to accept it, even though her parents tried to convince her that it was the only way to be a good Christian.

"You are so quiet, and what do you think?" asked Ivan.
"Do you think our Lord Jesus Christ wants us to live in poverty?" she asked.

"What makes you think that? At the moment, we have bigger problems than thinking about what Jesus Christ would want from us, don't you think?" he asked, a little surprised by this question.

"You know, we were lucky to arrive here safely, and now that we are in such a developed country, I can realise my visions."

"Yes, yes, you and your visions. Enjoy the view, and we have just arrived in Germany."

No matter who Viktoria tried to talk to about her visions, which she saw as a gift from God, they seemed not to be taken seriously. Even with her husband, Ivan, she could not talk about it, even though he came from a more modern family, since his parents had also emigrated to Germany in the 1960s to earn the money to build their house. His strict Catholic family had not brought him up in poverty, but he felt that Viktoria's horizons were far too wide for a woman.

At least, that was the culture he was brought up in and the patriarchal religion dictated by the Catholic Church, according to which men primarily exercise power. But Viktoria's spirit was utterly free to unfold and prosper, for she trusted what she felt, convinced that God had given her vocation, regardless of the fact that she was a woman. But the people around her kept confusing her, and she had to ask herself, as a believing Christian, whether it could be considered a sin for a person to desire prosperity.

But what does God think about people, especially women, striving for success?

Our society teaches us that men are still the ones who earn the most and are successful, but the Bible also speaks of the subordination of women to men, as in Ephesians 5:21,23.

'The one subdues the other in the common reverence of Christ...'.

Did this mean the wife was to do what the husband told her to do?

Well, with this phrase, Jesus certainly did not mean who had to do what to whom, but rather;

'Wives, submit to your husbands as to the Lord Christ. You men love your wives as Christ loved the Church and gave himself up for her to make her clean and holy in the water and by the Word'.

Simply put, love one another as Christ loved us and gave himself up for us as a gift and a sacrifice.

It may sound strange to many, but the Bible speaks of successful women, of the figure of the woman who is given a new dignity in the New Testament and a submissive and privileged element not in the hands but in the heart of Jesus. The woman of the New Testament has an advantage over the woman of the Old Testament: She receives and transmits liberation and healing. The Bible mentions several women from whose stories we can learn much, such as Iael, with her initiative and courage (Romans 15:4; 2 Timothy 3:16-17). Her story shows that God can direct events so that prophecies are fulfilled. Or Abigail, who, though beautiful and wealthy, had a balanced view of herself. For the sake of peace, she was willing to apologise for mistakes she had not made. Or Deborah, who was courageous and willing to make sacrifices. She encouraged others to do what was right in the eyes of God and did not hesitate to praise those who did the right thing. Queen

Ester is a magnificent example of courage, humility and modesty (Psalm 31:24; Philippians 2:3). Despite her beauty and position, she was not proud: She asked others for help and advice. When she turned to her husband, she spoke to him with tact and respect but also with openness.

Up to 21 women are mentioned in the Bible, some as positive examples, others as negative, like the woman of Lot. Her story illustrates the dangers of loving material things so much that we become disobedient to God. Jesus mentioned her as a negative example. He said: "Think of Lot's wife" (Luke 17:32).

But what does the Bible teach us about wealth, regardless of whether it is the woman or the man seeking success?

What did Viktoria know about success when she had been obsessed with it since childhood?

Viktoria did not know exactly what the Bible says about wealth because the books in the living rooms, including the Bible, were there to decorate the furniture. Anyone who knows a Croatian family knows that life takes place in the kitchen and that the living room is an inaccessible museum that is visited and admired only on great family occasions. Besides, good Christians should know what God wants for us because the priest regularly announces it in church during the service. But the message the priest had for the faithful was not the message that came from the depths of her heart. Even as a young girl, Viktoria tended to ask herself whether it was our God who wanted us to live in poverty through the example of Jesus' life or whether it was the Catholic Church that taught Christians to be poor. Questioning what the priest said was a provocation and a sin in her mother's eyes, and so she forced Viktoria to go to confession regularly.

But Viktoria was determined to be wealthy; that was what she felt deep down inside. There seemed to be an innate guiding voice within her, telling her to be wealthy and successful. But was that all this voice had to say to her?

Apparently not, for at some point, the same voice also guided her spiritual life and led her to turn away from the Catholic Church. During her transition from teenager to young woman, Viktoria often felt like she was in the wrong place at Mass. But the fact that she left the Catholic Church did not mean that she did not believe in God. She firmly believed in Him and Jesus Christ as the mediator between her and God. However, the God she believed in had nothing to do with the God represented by the Catholic Church. Hence, the idea of a God of love and abundance led her to attend a meeting of the Jehovah's Witnesses shortly before her twentieth birthday. She and her boyfriend at the time, Ivan, were both overwhelmed by their Catholic families and at a time when they did not know exactly what they wanted, they decided to go to this event secretly and without their parents' permission. So, after deceiving their parents, they met a family that was part of the event and got into their car. But on the way there, something happened that caused Viktoria to distance herself from this religion, even before she knew it.

During the drive to the venue, 100km away, they suddenly heard a loud bang, and the car began to sway from side to side. It all happened in a flash, as if in a dream, and she saw a wheel go into the embankment from the corner of her eye. Fear paralysed her body as she realised what had happened, and she could not utter a word. The car had lost one of its rear wheels. In those seconds of terror, she realised that this was probably going to be her last car ride and remained frozen and helpless, her back pressed to the seat. But then something happened, just as the driver screamed that he had lost control of the car. With a quick movement, the car pulled to the right as if it had been suddenly pushed, and the driver uttered a cry of despair. Then there was silence.

"My God!" muttered Viktoria in tears as the car suddenly stopped on the hard shoulder.

"Are you hurt?" asked Ivan, panicked, taking her in his arms.

"This is the punishment," she murmured.

Had this event meant something to them? Were Viktoria and Ivan being punished for having betrayed their parents?

As Christians, we will never be punished for our sins. This has already been done once and for all. 'There is no condemnation for those who are in Jesus Christ' (Romans 8:1). Through the sacrifice of Christ, God only sees the righteousness of Jesus Christ when He looks at us. Our sins have been nailed to the cross with Jesus, and we will never be punished for them.

Viktoria took this event very seriously and distanced herself from this religion.

As the years went by, her family saw her more and more as a rebel. She had visions of the future and talked about them openly. She dreamt of success and prosperity, stopped attending church, read the Gospel, and spent much time at her friend Ivan's house. Her parents were completely overwhelmed by her behaviour, her innate emancipation and her way of thinking, and they blamed her relationship with Ivan and forbade her to see him.

In an increasingly complicated family situation, after the sudden death of his father and because he, as the only son, felt obliged to support his mother financially, Ivan decided to go to his cousins in Germany to work while Viktoria stayed in Croatia. But suddenly, the war began, and after a few months, Ivan had to return to pick up Viktoria, who fled the country with only a few clothes in a bag.

"What the hell! Where have we ended up?" she asked herself when she saw a high-rise building in a suburb of Mannheim. Then the tram stopped.
"If you stop sleeping, we can get off; we have arrived at our flat," Ivan said.
"In our flat? At least 30 other families are living here. Are you sure?" she asked in surprise, remembering the lonely houses in her village and her parent's house with the vineyard in the garden.
"You'll soon get used to it," he replied simply.
"You've been staying here the last few months?" she asked in surprise.
"Yes."
Silently she followed him, certain that as a country girl, she would never get used to this living situation, while in her mind the vision of a house on the outskirts of town with lots of land, a vegetable garden, some fruit trees, a few goats, chickens and other animals were already forming.
Was her desire for prosperity too bold?

The Bible says in Ephesians (Eph 3:20) that God can do infinitely more than we can ask. Through the power of the Holy Spirit in us, God can do infinitely more than we can ask or understand. God is able. The Spirit is powerful. We, too, can be more than we can even imagine!

"This apartment is as small as our rabbit hutch," said Viktoria, looking at the 40-square-metre apartment.

"Small but nice," Ivan replied cheerfully.

"I'll never get used to so little space. I want to live in a house as soon as we are better off financially."

"Then I hope we win the lottery soon," he said amusedly.

"And I wish for success because, statistically, that is much more likely than winning the lottery!"

"May God bless all your plans for success, including possible failures, and encourage you to keep going, even if you are so persistent."

„He will," she thought.

After years of Viktoria expressing her desire to become a successful businesswoman, Ivan had no choice but to accept his newlywed's stubbornness.

But what does it mean to be successful in life?

For many, success is measured by results, whether in the economic, professional or academic sphere. For others, relationships with family, friends, and colleagues count. Those who serve God may feel that their success depends on their theocratic offices or their achievements in ministry. Each person has a different perspective and a different need for success and success experiences. Some people know exactly what kind of success they want, and others would like to be successful but do not know in what field. It is useful for these people to make a list of people they consider successful, admire, and respect and to see what qualities they have in common to find out what success means. Are these people rich, famous or influential? Are they socially active? Do they have many friends and a nice family? Our answers to these simple questions will show us what we carry in our hearts. And what we carry in our hearts greatly influences the decisions we make and the goals we pursue. - Luke 6:45.

But what about Ivan's heart? Did he have any? Or was it just Viktoria who wanted to succeed?

"I admire your ability to believe in success and, above all, to believe that God will help you to achieve it. You know, even though the world has become more modern in the 1990s, the fact remains that men are the ones who have the most power and make the most money. Women were created for other purposes."
"Aha, I see. And for what particular purpose was woman created, in your opinion?" she asked, confused.
"Well, when the Lord created woman, it was his sixth day of creation; he was working overtime; he must have been tired, and since women are known to be inexhaustible, he created one to help the man. For if woman was not created to help man and bear children, why was she created at all?"
"Tell me, are you stupid? Where exactly in the Bible did you find this information about women? You seem to be the only one in the world who neither seeks success nor happiness," she snapped angrily.

Obviously, Ivan was taking his cue from the patriarchal figure prescribed by the Catholic faith.

But God, our loving Father, wants us to find happiness and joy, regardless of the usual clichés of the Catholic Church. He sent us on earth to learn and progress through experiences, whether pleasant or painful. He leaves us free to choose between good and evil. Even Ivan, with his decision to leave Croatia and move to Germany, had shown that he had goals, even if he did not talk about them as openly and often as Viktoria.

But Viktoria had a different way of believing in her success, the fire of passion burning in her even when everyone around her doubted it, no matter how steep the road was. 'Ultimately, the fire comes from God Himself (Heb 12:29; Dan 7:9-10)'.

She believed in God's plan even though she did not know all the answers.

Most people yearn for success, but many do not even try to become successful because they are afraid of making mistakes or failing, even though we have everything we need to succeed. They excuse themselves by saying they have bad luck or that God does not want them to succeed. Most of the time, it is not God who does not believe in us, but we ourselves, and this is the only reason why we often do not achieve our goals or experience success. Sometimes, arrogance also prevents us from succeeding or makes us lose our success.

Even in the Bible, we find such quotations;

'The plans of an industrious man will certainly lead to wealth, but he who is too hasty will only fall into misfortune.'

Well, today, in the 21st century. First of all, it has to be said that the constant bombardment of the mass media feeds the desire for immediate success. If you are not successful, you will be rejected by society. All possibilities for earning money are offered with enticing advantages and tricks, which are so convincingly formulated that they give young people, in particular, the idea that everything can be achieved immediately, without difficulty, without long waiting periods and, most importantly, without any service in return. These tempting offers of extraordinary employment opportunities lead people to believe that everything is within reach without the need for effort, diligence and perseverance.

Whereas some people were educated about poverty in the past, today, prosperity has almost become an obligation. However, this distorted view of existence and this intoxication with easy success are only an illusion, for they create social, moral, and spiritual problems that are at the root of all the terrible realities of the world in which we live. Ours is a 'sick' society, full of anxieties and unhappiness, contrary to the much-praised theories according to which the individual would reach the summit of serenity and happiness if he had a more comfortable life, lived in more comfortable houses, worked less and with less effort, and finally avoided difficulties more and more. None of this gives us the feeling that success brings something positive. But if success also brings negative things, is it right to desire it at all?

Well, before we can answer this question, we must first define the meaning of the word "success." A well-known dictionary describes success as "a favourable event or successful outcome of an enterprise." If this is the definition, then there is also a guarantee of success for those who believe in Christ, for the Bible says of the divine wisdom, which many commentators take to be a type of Christ himself: "Wisdom and good success are mine..." (Proverbs 8:14). This verse contains at least three truths: The Lord is the author of success; success is the result of accepting His advice; there are successes that are not 'good'.

Only success that comes from God is good; others are not desirable. This verse, which must be regarded as fundamental on this subject, was written through the inspiration of the Holy Spirit by a man who had success such as perhaps only a few others have achieved in their earthly existence: King Solomon. He, 'wiser than any other man,' asked God for wisdom, and God gave him wealth (1 Kings 4:31). He recognised that 'good success' only comes from 'divine wisdom'. This 'success,' however, is not what is commonly understood in the world. It is not a 'fortunate event' but a 'good success,' in this sense, success is guaranteed to all who have accepted Jesus Christ as their Saviour and Lord and follow Him faithfully.

Thinking of the many verses in the Bible, we can say that no verse says: 'Be a fool and success is sure'.

When Viktoria came to Germany in 1991, she immediately started looking for work. Being in a multicultural country, she saw no reason to let her lack of language skills stop her. So she started working in Croatian restaurants and tailor shops, where she had the opportunity to learn German in direct contact with the public.

"What language do you speak?" asked Ivan, amused.

"German," replied Viktoria.

"You think so," Ivan grinned.

"I can't deny that there are situations where I have the feeling that I'm not learning fast enough, and that's very frustrating, and especially at work, there are also many funny situations, like when the words were spoken in reverse order and got a completely different meaning than the one they were supposed to have. But I don't get discouraged that easily."

"Yes, I understand that. In the beginning, I always had my Croatian-English dictionary with me when I went shopping so that I could translate the names of the groceries and communicate at the checkout. I also had a lot of trouble with the Deutschmark, so I had to struggle with exchanging money. And like everyone else, I had to attend doctor's appointments and deal with paperwork at the local council because you can only stay in Germany with a residence permit, and you can only get one if you work," he says.

"I did not think about all these things when I was still in Croatia. I did not know what was waiting for me, but I knew I would take this chance.

The will to succeed proved stronger than the obstacles. Was it also good to set goals as a Christian?

The answer is simple: Yes, it is good to have goals! Jesus also had goals. God wants us to live with a purpose, not randomly. The fact that we ask questions and seek His will means we want to make good use of this life. His Word will help us to have the right goals and to stay motivated to achieve them.

But do not expect the Bible to give you a list of things to do or a quick formula for outlining goals. If it were that simple, we could read the list, wipe it away and never talk to God about our plans. This is not about following rules but about having a relationship with the One who created you and gave you unique gifts and talents to use: God Himself.

Chapter 2 Living disconnected

"I feel like I need to throw up," Viktoria said with a pale face, holding her hand to her mouth.

"I'm unsurprised because you will have skipped lunch again in your zeal to work."

"You're talking nonsense!"

"And you only live for work!"

"I have a late period..." Viktoria added.

"See? I always say that stress is the root of all evil," said Ivan, convinced.

"And love is the heart of creation," she added.

"But all this has to do with work. Have you lost your mind because of all the overtime?"

"I'm pregnant..."

Exactly four months after her 23rd birthday, Viktoria discovered she was pregnant. What she had told her friends as a young girl, and for which she had been ridiculed, had come true: at the age of three and twenty, she was expecting her first child. Was it a coincidence?

"You seem to be both stressful and funny today. You take the pill; how can you be pregnant?" asked Ivan, amused. But then she took something out of her pocket and handed it to him.

"What is this weird stick?" asked Ivan.

"It's a positive pregnancy test. I did it at work."

"Oh, shit!" he replied.

She, the rebel, the black sheep in her circle of friends and family, had turned away from religion and was making progress in her life plan. Should she not be less respected in the eyes of God? With perseverance, she followed this voice despite the obstacles and fears placed in her path by those around her. This stubbornness to be different drove away some people in her life, even in her career, over the years, but in return for the people who left her, others believed in her and magically took her to the next level. She came across as a determined black sheep who knew exactly what she wanted. She was considered a black sheep even though she had done no harm to others, simply because she did not do what others told her to do.

"Why do I have to be normal and inconspicuous if I can be the best?"

Viktoria always asked herself when people around her told her to be realistic because she felt she had the right to expect success and not be afraid of achieving it.

"Is 'oh, shit!' all you have to say?" she asked impatiently.

"We are only 23 and 25 and have only been in Germany for a few years. We have no family to support us. Besides, you want to make a career. How can that work?" he asked, astonished.

"Are you serious? We are a family! Besides, we live in a country full of opportunities, and I have no intention of spending the rest of my life as a housewife just because I have children. Becoming a mother will not jeopardise my career opportunities; I have enough strength to do both jobs perfectly. Nor can I extinguish my burning desire for success, for it is within me; I feel prosperity and wealth deep within me; it is a gift from God that will sooner or later show itself outwardly."

"Oh, Viktoria! We were born in a different country and taught different values. I feel rooted in my values and traditions. When women give birth, they devote themselves entirely to the family. Even the priest used to say in the services that women today are becoming increasingly rebellious and are fighting for more equality!"

"Yes, exactly, the Catholic Church. You seem to have forgotten why I refused to go to church. Ephesians 5:21-33 says that men and women must submit to one another out of respect for Christ. The Catholic Church has been trying to restrict women's rights in Croatia for years. I do not have to be in Germany to know that men do not stand at the top because women also have rights! Everyone knows that the ultra-patriarchal organisation of the Vatican, together with the Islamic states, has been trying for years to restrict the rights and freedoms of women. The God I believe in is a God of love, not a God of restrictions. He is a God of the living and not of the dead! Mark 12."

"Are you listening to yourself? You are newly pregnant, and your hormones are playing havoc. You sound like an emancipated feminist!"

Although both Viktoria and Ivan had distanced themselves from the Catholic Church in the past, at some point, Ivan's spiritual development came to a standstill. He seemed neither to hear nor heed the inner guidance Viktoria had felt and followed since childhood. Both read the Gospel over a long period of time, but while Viktoria followed her clear spiritual path after leaving the Catholic Church, Ivan fell back into the old pattern. This led to different ways of thinking and arguments between the two.

"Are these the basic values you want to pass on to our children?" she asked seriously.
"Each of us passes on the values given to us," he replied.
"That will cause problems, and I can see it coming! Because in our family, there will be no more generations growing up with an education based on poverty or the oppression of women," she replied confidently.

After a few years in Germany, Ivan seemed to have forgotten his wife's true nature, namely that Viktoria had rejected a certain kind of parental upbringing from an early age. This rejection earned her the title of 'black sheep'. Such an upbringing would have found no place in her own family life, for she was born with the genes for success. Hard-working and without wasting a day, Viktoria began to work when she arrived in Germany. Without the internet, without Google, in a foreign country and with a language barrier, she found a job just one day after her arrival. Did she expect to be welcomed with open arms when she arrived in Germany? No, of course not. When Ivan arrived in Germany before the start of the Croatian War, the first plans for Viktoria began.
Every day when he left the house, whether it was to go to the supermarket or to work, Ivan noted the company names that might suit Viktoria as a beginner. And so it was that Viktoria

arrived in Germany and went straight to a Croatian tailor the next day to ask for a job.

Can one say that fortune was waiting for her with open arms?

Well, when you consider that between 1991 and 1994, shortly before the birth of her first child, Viktoria had done all sorts of jobs, from maid to cleaner, nurse, seamstress, and finally, a saleswoman in a Croatian grocery store because her German was not good enough to find another job, you can say that she worked like hell.

But the birth of her second child marked a turning point, and in 1997, she took a job at Lidl, which she left in 2001 to take a better-paid job in an electronics store. During this time, she took several computer courses, which enabled her to get a job as a clerk at BASF in Ludwigshafen in 2002.

Her dreams were fulfilled after 11 years of hard work in Germany. She finally found an office job in a world-famous company and became a businesswoman, exactly the woman she had seen in her childhood visions and told her friends about.

In the same year she celebrated her 32nd birthday, she realised her visions as a child in a foreign country, with a foreign language and far away from her family.

In the first 11 years of her life in Germany, Viktoria worked her way through all the stations, changing jobs each time she reached the next stage of her development, becoming a mother of two children, taking part in further education programmes and then reaching her zenith at BASF in Ludwigshafen am Rhein as a sales assistant. Her friends, who also had a migrant background, were enthusiastic and jealous. But inside, she knew that she could have achieved more, and perhaps she also felt the need to prove herself after growing up in an economically tense environment.

Was it right to want to dare more? What does our God think about the fact that we humans have the need to prove ourselves, and what does the Bible say about the need to prove ourselves?

We all want to be accepted by others. Even children learn to read the signals of those they want to please and adjust their behaviour accordingly. But if we look to the opinions of others for most of our affirmation and self-esteem, we are on the wrong track because people's opinions change all the time. If we give them too much importance, we will be constantly disappointed. For example, if we seek popularity as a means to happiness, we practise idolatry. If we find our personal worth in something or someone other than God, we create an idol, something we use to satisfy deep, heartfelt desires that only God can fulfil. But if we do what we like, do it only for ourselves, and do it with passion, then we will succeed on all levels.

Galatians 1:10 says, 'Do I seek the approval of men or the approval of God? Or do I seek to please men? For if I still seek to please men, I am not a servant of Jesus Christ'. According to this verse, we cannot please God and the world at the same time.
In her haste to prove what she was capable of,
Viktoria soon found herself in a one-way street, trapped in a marriage that was all about competition. And the children were

the spectators. The romantic relationship soon turned into a race for more money as Ivan developed a passion for management positions. Eventually, her job at BASF could no longer keep up with her husband's income, so she took weekend courses, founded her own real estate company in 2012 and left BASF.

With the incredible number of orders coming in during the real estate boom, Viktoria felt she was in the right place at the right time. She had never seen such gigantic sales in her life. Full of enthusiasm but also plagued by a sense of guilt towards the families, some of whom could not afford such sums, she wrote out ludicrous invoices after the notaries' appointments. Soon, she was considered very rich by her family and friends. The people around her appreciated her, her clients loved her work, and she became part of a new social class overnight. But as time went on, the hours became harder and harder, and they were compensated by what they could afford with the money. They bought property to rent out, went on increasingly expensive holidays, sometimes to places where their children would be bored, and returned home frustrated after two weeks. Worst of all, the more they earned, the more money they needed to live, so eventually, their lives revolved around work.

Everything led to a constant struggle, so within a short time, she found herself in a toxic relationship. The more months went by, the more she lacked energy, her mind was empty, she had no creativity, and it was only five years after she had begun to be independent that she felt a kind of disgust for it because she began to realise that she had lost her freedom and that she was beginning to lose herself. She had completely cut herself off from everything, from herself, from her family and from God. But this did not scare her, for her standard of living was now so high that she had no choice but to continue to work tirelessly, so much so that her body, after several physical 'warning signs' that she ignored, rebelled. Her breasts had to be removed because of fast-growing tumours. She was successful, people admired her, and she earned a lot of money, but she became ill. How could this happen?

"Anyone who seeks success without thinking of God and his family is a loser," she heard on the radio on her way to another doctor's appointment after her mastectomy.

In a situation as dramatic as her illness, she realised that it was good for her to stop and reflect for a while;
'What is my life's path direction, and where am I going?'
The so-called 'theology of affluence' has spread in recent decades across all social classes. We were created to live in abundance, joy, peace and prosperity. Faith in God is the means to health, wealth, success and earthly power.
And she, too, adapted her life more and more to this theology. After all, she was programmed for success from childhood, for God was her silent coach. But why, then, did she become ill if God, with divine right, wants to secure health, economic prosperity and social success for the believers?

In our world, where everything is for sale, even religious life follows a commercial logic of exchange with God, and the great emphasis is on the possession of material goods and health as a visible sign of faith in God. Whoever converts to Jesus "overcomes the curse of the law" (Gal 3:13-14), including sickness and poverty, as Deuteronomy 28 says. Christ has the right to material goods and health as a visible sign of faith in God. Christ has the right to have the best on this earth, including a nice new car, clothes, luxury living, and enjoying everything the consumer world offers. The motto was invented for those who have developed a bad conscience towards the poor: "If you give your share to your church, God will bless you with success and abundance. If you do not get what you want, it means that you have little faith, and if you do not pay your share, you will remain tied to the devil and live in misery."

In the past, Viktoria was taught to be poor because the Catholic Church said that only the poor had pure hearts and could be accepted by God. Today, mankind is taught to be rich based on the new theology of wealth.

Was Viktoria's success also doomed because she officially left the Catholic Church when she set up her company to save on taxes? Did God think she had acted out of greed and punished her with illness?
Viktoria had not felt a part of the Catholic Church since she was a young girl and had decided to leave it officially sooner or later. Could she conclude from this that God had punished her with a delay? Had she incurred God's wrath and been punished with illness?

How could it be that after years of great visions in which she felt God's presence in everything she did, she suddenly lost her health? Was God no longer looking after her?

Who does not need reassurance in times of uncertainty and trial? Who is so sure of himself that he does not need encouragement that gives him stability in life?

At the moment when Viktoria felt fragile and needed God's guidance and presence more than anything else, she no longer felt him; she no longer felt his presence. But, to be honest, she had not thought of him or sought him for a long time. She had literally forgotten him. Even her visions had disappeared, she had no new goals, everything revolved around her physical recovery, she had to function, and she just wanted to get well quickly so that she could work, for as a self-employed real estate agent, she had not only the privilege of writing large bills but also many monthly expenses that had to be covered. She was caught up in a struggle to make money, meet her commitments, maintain the car and pay for holidays. She felt like a machine that had to run at all costs, completely isolated from herself. She had lost herself.

'If I am cut off from myself, how can I connect with God? Impossible,' she thought to herself.

Since the fundamental goal of our life is personal growth and success, there must be moments of trial and difficulty that allow us to develop. But Viktoria felt completely cut off from this development.

The only thing she felt was the tests she underwent, and like all the other "warning signs", she ignored them and continued to fight for her job, lurching from one misfortune to another for several years, undergoing several breast operations so that she could hardly go to work, and losing everything she had built up within two years. Her marriage did not survive either. She spent days and weeks wondering why. It felt like a nightmare or, rather, death. In the five years she worked as a self-employed real estate agent, she managed to build up what some people could not after 40 years of hard work, and in the following two years, she lost everything. A storm had shattered her life.

But it was in that moment of deep darkness that she began to feel something inside, just as she found herself alone and in poor health. Alone and facing financial disaster, she felt a kind of inner peace, a kind of relief and release. What had happened to her? Had she already lost everything and felt relieved, almost grateful for it? Had she lost her mind?

There were days on which she wished she could rely on a certain will of God as her vocation. How reassuring and comforting it would have been, in times of doubt and difficulty, to know that this was part of God's eternal plan, in which every element of her life, whether happy or sad, would find its place and purpose! But at the same time, something stirred in her, and she had to ask herself:

Would God present us with a plan to be fulfilled that was outside of us without giving us even a sure means of recognising it?

If words have a meaning, if we also speak of God's will, what loss would this divine will not mean for our freedom? And what suffering it would be for us if we had to decide: Every mistake, every delay would be dramatic. We will lose everything if we run parallel to God's plan and unwillingly place ourselves outside His plan. This is all the more true as we know that God's ways are not our ways, and we experience every day how difficult and sometimes risky it is to discern what we call God's will. To say that God has placed us at a crossroads, where we have several directions, only one of which is the good one, without giving us the means to discern it with certainty, would correspond to the image of a perverted God and could in no way express the attitude of the God of the Covenant, who came to save the lost.

However, We are aware that it is God who calls us by name and that our encounter with him holds a special path for us. From Abraham to Peter, the history of salvation is full of examples of people called to a new life for a specific mission, often symbolised by a name change: "From now on you shall be called Abraham, Israel, Peter." The mission of Moses, Jeremias or Paul seems to correspond to a specific will of God, even to the point of marking their lives with a singularity that leads them into solitude. Exceptional destinies or examples of what we are all called to live?

In these dark moments, however, one thing became clear to Viktoria: The path she had taken in the last few years before her illness was not something she had done for herself but to please others: her friends, her family, her husband's family and her husband himself. She had embarked on this path to assert herself, to prove herself, not to do something for herself, but to do something that would make her deeply happy. But as soon as she was free of all that, including her husband and family, something profound changed in her. She no longer had to put dinner on the table at 7 p.m., she no longer had to sell three properties a month to stay competitive, she no longer had to spend her free time in places that were not relaxing or even stressful, she no longer had to be perfect all the time, and she no longer had to strive to please others to be enough. She felt complete, even if she had nothing. From that moment on, something happened, and she began to feel herself touched by small things like the sight of a sunset, and she began to feel that she was no longer alone.

The God she found herself facing was not this extraordinarily powerful computer, capable of programming and storing billions of individual destinies in its memory, which we should consult with fear and trembling about our future. It was love that took the risk of bringing us to life, in similarity and diversity, to offer us union and community.

We must turn to this vision of God if we can stand before God's will in truth. Then, we will no longer recognise him as a judgment or a condemnation but as an invitation to participate. The hope of creating something new with him, his call for a new creation, awakened hope in Viktoria in the darkest time of her life. She realised that our choices do not come out of nowhere but are prepared with the material that makes up the human character: our temperament and our history. We cannot do everything, but we can give meaning and a face to what would be nothing but fate. In this effort of personal creation, in response to the call of God, the Spirit comes to us, not as an external force, but as an inner energy awakened in us by the acceptance of the Word of God.

The answer we will give to God is not written anywhere in the Book of Life or the Heart of God except as expectation and hope. Hope in that which God does not yet see and to which we will give shape and face. It is the greatness and the risk of our lives that we are called to awaken God's joy through the quality and generosity of our response.

The Word of God will not dictate our choices but will open our horizons: "It has been said, I tell you: Seek ye first the kingdom of God, and his righteousness" (Matthew 5:26; 6:33). "The will of my Father is that you bear fruit and that your fruit remains" (John 14:3; 15:16).

Since the Bible often speaks of blessings, one wonders whether there is a special will of God for each of us, regardless of the difficulties we must overcome on our journey through life. A defeat, an encounter, a transfer... How can we accept something that we have not decided on or even brings us into an imbalance? How can we accept his help when we are in need? Why does he sometimes not seem to listen to us when we need him?

Well, God wants us to give him space, to long for him, so that he can come to us. If we think we do not need God, who reaches out to us through Jesus Christ, because we think we are sufficient for ourselves, then we are on the way to failure. God loves to be sought.

God wants to be sought because God is a gift. He is the absolute gift because he is love, and love will give everything and give itself.

Luke 11:5-13

Ask, and it will be given to you; seek, and you will find; knock, and it will be opened to you. For whoever asks receives; whoever seeks finds; and whoever knocks, the door will be opened to him.

How can we ask for help without taking Jesus Christ into our boat? Like James and John, who cried out to God: "Lord, we are lost, do you care? In the same way, Viktoria experienced the events of her life as an injustice.

To the panic-stricken apostles, the Lord replied: "Why are you afraid? Why have you no faith?"

What prevents us from making an act of faith in God, accepting that we do not understand everything at once, and trusting in Him who "obeys the wind and the sea"?

If, like the apostles in the Gospel of Mark, we take Jesus into the little boat of our life, because to take Jesus means to believe in him who can do everything. His strength will enable us to withstand all storms, face all evil winds, and reach the other shore with him. Trusting in God is the key to success in life because he never abandons us.

We know in faith that the Lord is always with us. But how often do we find it difficult to listen or pray to Him? Some people say: "I cannot connect with God." This is a painful experience that can lead us to give up prayer. Perhaps this happened to us. Sometimes, although we try very hard, even if we have done it for years, the feeling remains that we do not know how to speak with God. Although we are sure we have a direct line to Him, we do not overcome the inner monologue. We do not achieve that intimacy for which we are so longing.

In this century of stress and social media, we should not only be concerned about not losing the connection to the Internet but also about keeping the connection to God active, which means not interrupting the dialogue, listening to Him and telling Him our things. How can we stay awake at the other end of the line? What can we do so that our prayer is a dialogue between two persons? How can we deepen our intimacy with the Lord over the years? For this, we must keep our spirit alive.

God the Father made the plan of salvation. The Son of God accomplished redemption through his cross sacrifice and resurrection. The Holy Spirit brings this redemption to us and does much more. The Holy Spirit is of fundamental importance to Christian life. His task is to make us see Jesus Christ. He is never the centre of attention. In the New Testament, for example, no prayers to the Holy Spirit exist. He is mentioned much, much less than Christ and the Father. Yet his role is fundamental. One of the functions of the Holy Spirit in our lives is to unite us with God, for it is important that we do not extinguish His work in us. The word of God comes from the Holy Spirit.

Take also the helmet of salvation and the sword of the Spirit, which is the word of God. (Ephesians 6:17)
The Holy Spirit strengthens us and enables us to overcome the trials of life. It is His power that works in us. (Romans 15:13).

Now, the God of hope, fill you with all joy and peace in faith so that you may abound in hope through the power of the Holy Spirit. (Rom 15:13)

This power of the Spirit working in us enables us to do what we could not do on our own. An example is Paul telling the church in Corinth how to deal with a man in sin.

The word of God has also been given to us through the Holy Spirit. What a great blessing!

Chapter 3 God's Existence

"Where is your God when you need him?" asked Annika as Viktoria sat crying and helpless on the sofa.

"I think God wants us to seek him always, not just when we need something from him. You know, I used to have a very different kind of relationship with God. I think that is why my life has been so good for so many years," Viktoria replied.

"Is there a God at all?" asked Annika, who was tired of seeing her friend Viktoria in this situation.

"I think so; at least, I have felt it for years because I am sure that the voice inside me that has guided me since childhood was God's voice. In recent times, on some days, I have had the feeling that I hear this voice within me, but I do not know if I am imagining it because my life is in a storm at the moment. I pray that He helps me to get rid of all these problems in the name of Jesus Christ. But my world continues to shatter, and I do not know how much longer I can bear it. Does God, our Father, not see how much I suffer? Why does he do nothing to help me?" asked Viktoria, disheartened.

"Now you know why we are atheists.

That was the dry answer from Viktoria's friend Annika, who had been there for her all these years, especially during the worst phases of her illness and financial catastrophe. Annika was the only one in her circle of friends who was not only there when it came to crazy parties or expensive presents.

"Is there proof of the existence of God? And can science exclude the existence of God?" asked Annika quite directly before Viktoria could say anything about atheists.

"For the faithful, the existence of God does not require any proof or justification, and they are sure that the divine nature only reveals itself to those who are ready to receive it, but it is proven that there are also many atheists or people of other religions who in the course of their lives have felt the need to read the Bible, some of them have completely converted to Christ, others only shortly before their death, and still others have never done so. Maybe one day you will," replied Viktoria, but this was not the kind of answer Annika, an atheist, had expected. Rather, she was referring to concrete evidence for the existence of God.

Everything in this world has a cause, including the universe. Why is there something instead of nothing? Science, which has succeeded in refuting the theory of the universe as "intelligent design," cannot yet answer this question, which many theoretical physicists are increasingly asking. To do so, people would first have to better understand the laws of nature and their origins. Anyone who thinks impartially about the universe's existence cannot help but ask himself the question of its origin. When we witness certain events, we instinctively ask for their causes. Why should we not ask this question of all the beings and phenomena we discover in the world? When we speak of proofs of the existence of God, we must stress that these are not proofs of a scientific-experimental nature. In the modern sense of the word, scientific proofs apply only to things that can be perceived with the senses, for only these can the instruments of investigation and verification that science uses be applied. To strive for scientific proof of the existence of God would be to reduce God to the rank of the beings of our world and thus to be methodically mistaken about what God is. Science must recognise its limits and its inability to reach the existence of God: It can neither confirm nor deny this existence. This does not mean, however, that scientists are incapable of finding convincing reasons for recognising God's existence in their scientific studies. If science, as such, cannot reach God, then the scientist, who possesses an intelligence whose object is not limited to sensual things, can discover in the world reasons for the affirmation of a Being that transcends him. Many scientists have made this discovery or are in the process of making it.

Some scientists even dare to say that God is science, especially when understanding and explaining phenomena without scientific explanation. However, all observations concerning the development of life lead to a similar conclusion. The development of living beings, the stages of which science is trying to determine and the mechanisms it is trying to discover display an inner finalism that arouses admiration. This finality, which directs living beings in a direction for which they are neither master nor responsible, forces us to accept a Spirit who is the inventor, the creator.

Is there then a definitive proof for the existence of God?

The answer to this question depends very much on what a "final" proof means. Can we touch or see God as we can touch and see people? No. Nor can we touch or see the wind; we do not even know where it comes from, but we can feel it. The fact that God is Spirit means that God our Father does not have a human body, so He sent His Son, Jesus Christ, to the earth to teach the truth. Jesus proclaimed the Kingdom of God, a heavenly government that would bring peace to the whole earth. He offered people the hope of eternal life. (John 4:14; 18:36, 37). He also gave many counsels on how to find true happiness. (Matthew 5:3; 6:19-21) He also taught by example. He showed how to do God's will even under difficult circumstances. When he was mistreated, he did not seek revenge. Peter 2:21-24.

Jesus taught his apostles a love based on selflessness. In humble obedience to the Father, he gave up his extraordinary position in heaven and came down to earth to live among men. No one could have taught us better what love is than Jesus. John 15:12, 13; Philippians 2:5-8. Independently of the scientific explanation of the existence of God, there are 1093 prophecies in the Bible referring to Jesus Christ and His Church, and every single one of them has been fulfilled! The Old Testament contains 48 prophecies referring to the crucifixion of Jesus. Because several prophets, living in different communities over the course of 1000 years, made predictions 500 years before Jesus Christ, the probability of these prophecies coming true simply exceeds our wildest imaginings.

One of the insights Viktoria had gained since her illness was that it is not enough to know that God exists when hard times come but that the relationship with God must be constantly nurtured. She had discovered the connection and the way to God as a child. Most people wonder why He does not come to our aid when we are in need. Many of us do not realise until later, or after years, that the moment that seemed to take our lives was actually a new beginning. One of the most difficult aspects of the Christian life is the fact that being a Christian does not make us immune to the trials and tribulations of life. As in all things, God's ultimate goal is for us to grow more and more into the image of his Son (Rom 8:29). This is the goal of the Christian, and everything in life, including trials and tribulations, is designed to enable us to achieve this goal.

They are part of the process of sanctification: We are being set apart for God's purposes and enabled to live for His glory. The effect of trials is explained in 1 Peter 1:6-7: "Therefore rejoice, even though for a little while you may be afflicted with many trials, so that the testing of your faith, which is much more precious than gold, which perishes even when it is tried in the fire, may lead to glory, honour and glory in the revelation of Jesus Christ." The true believer's faith is strengthened by the trials we experience so that we can live in the certainty that it is genuine and will last forever.

Trials develop a godly character that leads us to 'glorify' ourselves in tribulation because we know that tribulation produces perseverance, perseverance produces experience, and experience produces hope. "Hope does not confuse us, because the love of God has been poured into our hearts by the Holy Spirit who has been given to us" (Rom 5:3-5). Jesus Christ has given us the perfect example. "God shows his love for us in that Christ died for us while we were still sinners" (Romans 5:8). These verses reveal aspects of God's divine purpose, both for the trials and sufferings of Jesus Christ and for our own. Holding fast to the faith proves our faith. "I can do all things through Christ who strengthens me" (Php 4:13). However, we must be careful not to excuse our 'trials and tribulations' resulting from our wrong behaviour. "Let no one among you suffer as a murderer, a thief or an evildoer, or because he interferes in the affairs of others" (1 Peter 4:15). God will forgive us our sins because the eternal penalty for them was paid by the sacrifice of His Son Jesus Christ on the cross. Nevertheless, we must suffer the natural consequences of our sins and wrong decisions in this life. But God even uses these sufferings to shape us for His purposes and our highest good.

All we have to do is to join Him.

But how do we find our way to God if we have lost the connection? Well, the Good News is that God is always online in the dark hours, in the sunny hours, when the storm is raging and when the sun's rays are caressing the petals of a flower. Our relationship with God has no communication problems or interruptions except for those we deliberately cause. To enter into a relationship with God, one must seek Him and prepare to receive Him, just as a young man in love prepares to meet the girl he loves.

At some point, in the dark moments of illness and financial disaster, Viktoria also realised that she had lost her connection with God, especially in times when she did not need Him, when she could experience success and prosperity, and when she herself felt like God. During the storm, she noticed that she was missing more and more the feeling she had had as a teenager, that strong feeling of belonging completely to God, of wanting to feel His presence all the time, of wanting to be intimate with Him, and of having a feeling of fullness in her chest, as if her heart was about to explode. Often, people do not see that problems exist for us to learn something, reconsider our decisions, change our ways, and reconnect with ourselves and our deepest desires because God has a special will for each one of us.

In the Old Testament, there is a story about a man named Abraham. In Genesis 12:1 it says that God asked Abraham to leave his homeland and go to a place that He would show him. Leave one's own country and homeland to go to a place where one has still heard nothing? That sounds pretty scary! But Genesis 12:4 says: "Abraham went out as the Lord had told him...."

God never gave Abraham the whole plan. He left more details than Abraham had intended. Rather, God gave Abraham instructions for the immediate steps he should take. It was on the same basis of trust that Viktoria left her country, Croatia, to go to Germany, guided by the little voice within her.

"I know no one who is as positive and generous as you, so I cannot understand what has happened to you," Annika said to Viktoria with a veil of sympathy.

"There must be a reason for this; I cannot and will not imagine anything else," Viktoria said defensively.

"Such nonsense! What good is it? What good is suffering?" cried Annika.

"Even Jesus Christ had to suffer when crucified to save us!" replied Viktoria.

"You are my best friend, and I love you very much, so I am not allowed to say what I think about all this."

"I love you too, and I know you will understand if I disagree with you."

Although Viktoria appreciated her friend Annika very much and was grateful for everything she did for her, she realised that it was not always easy to be friends with someone who questioned the existence of something greater, especially when that something was the Almighty God. This kind of disagreement, and the fact that Viktoria did not accept what the Catholic Church prescribed, was also a source of conflict during her marriage to Ivan. Although Viktoria had lost her connection to God in her later years, she could never have imagined that one day she would question His existence. While Ivan believed in God and even remained faithful to what the Catholic Church expected of him, Annika denied God.

In recent years, however, the subject of God has become more and more a matter of public interest, not least because of the many young people who have become followers of Jesus Christ. Young people follow the example of other young Christians in social media and proclaim the Word of God. Others post live how they are baptised in a pond. It seems to be coming back into fashion that you can communicate with God through Jesus Christ. Jesus as the subject of songs has become very popular among young people in recent years: Think of the success of music and film productions such as Green's Godspell, Rice and Jewison's Jesus Christ Superstar, Tony Cucchiara's Cain and Abel and Townshend and Ken Russell's Tommy. The new generation sees Jesus as the greatest revolutionary because his revolution challenges structures and methods. In Christ, they find all that is sublime in man; in him, they find their noblest aspirations, their highest ideals. In him, they also find the true proof of his life.

" I am the way, the truth and the life" (John 14:6).

In addition to the historical texts, there are also physical proofs of the existence of Jesus Christ, the Incarnate Word, the true God and the true man. These are connected, for example, with the oldest archaeological find, the so-called Nazareth inscription, and there is also archaeological evidence for the existence of Pontius Pilate and other persons mentioned in the Gospels.

When we speak of Jesus of Nazareth, we refer to the historical figure who lived in the vicinity of modern-day Israel between 0 and 33 AD. But how can we be sure that Jesus really lived, and from when until when did he live? In addition to the well-known sources, including the Gospels, there are various non-Christian writings from the first two centuries, especially Jewish and Roman texts, which speak of the existence of Jesus.

The Syrian Stoic philosopher Mara Bar Serapion, the Samaritan historian Thallus, and the official Roman historians Pliny, Tacitus and Suetonius wrote that He was an intelligent man who could reach and convince people by his preaching," "He had a brother named James," "He gathered followers around him," "He performed miracles and changed the appearance of the Jews," "He was called king and Messiah," "He worked within the framework of the Jewish religion and soon beyond," "He died a violent death due to condemnation by the authorities."

Also, the texts of the historian Flavius, now known as the 'Antiquitates,' in which Flavius writes around 93 AD.
At this time, there lived Jesus, a very wise man," which confirms the existence of Jesus.
If we ask ourselves: "Why do we believe in God?" then the first answer is our faith: God has revealed Himself to human beings and has come into contact with them. The supreme revelation of God came to us in Jesus Christ, God made man. We believe in God because God has allowed himself to be discovered by us as the highest being, as the great "Existent One." God certainly speaks to us in a thousand ways. God speaks softly but constantly in the Holy Scripture - especially in the Gospels - and also in us. God speaks to us. Unceasingly. He speaks in words and also in deeds. His language is much richer than ours. For example, he can evoke hidden resources within us by using people or what is happening around us.
God speaks by acting on our personal powers, which He can move from within: to our intellect through inspiration, to our emotions through affection, to our will through purpose. Often, God speaks directly to the heart, whose language He knows best. He does this through the deep desires that He Himself sows. Listening to God, therefore, often consists of exploring our hearts and having the courage to present our desires to Him to discern what helps us do His will and what does not.

"Do you think, after all you are going through, that there is a God or not?" asked Annika provocatively.

"I think that all that we are going through does not define who we are, and it certainly does not define our identity, but it simply defines a time, a season that will pass, and there is one thing that will remain forever, and that is His goodness and His faithfulness. If we do not understand the reason for what we are going through, then we should know that we are not called to understand everything but to always trust. What distinguishes us and makes us God's children is and remains his grace."

Red in the face and with eyes that were about to burst from their caves, Annika got up from her chair, slapped her hand on the table and shouted, "But your bad season has been going on for three damned years!"

Chapter 4   God's revelation

W hen you walk through the water, I am with you; when you walk through the streams, they will not sweep you away. When you walk through the fire, you will not be crushed; no flame will burn you.

With these verses from Isaiah 43:2, Viktoria began the day.

"Mum, we agreed to meet to discuss a possible move, but you have already dismantled most of the furniture and packed the contents into boxes. What is going on here?" asked Luka, Viktoria's older son.

"Well, I already have a buyer for our house; the viewing is in three weeks," Viktoria replied.

"What, you have a buyer for our house? But where will you live then?" asked her youngest son, Marko.

"Perhaps you have forgotten that I have been living alone in a house of over 200 square metres for months. At the moment, I would be happy with an 80 square metre apartment..."

"But you are no longer used to living in a flat. What are your plans? Are you going to live near us? I mean, where will we do our training?" asked Luka, hoping to find out what his mother was planning.

"I'm going to move to southern Germany, near the Swiss border."

"To the Swiss border?" asked Marko.

Marko and Luka looked at each other in surprise and disbelief, their faces contorted. The dream villa with its park-like garden, where they had lived with his family for twelve years, the villa of their dreams, for which they had sacrificed so much, had been exchanged for the desire for a new start.

"I know this decision may seem strange to you, but I must leave this place. The voice of my heart is strong and insistent, and you know that even as a child, I had a heart that listened to God's instructions."

"Do you take such a step only because of what your heart tells you? But you know no one there, and you are 250 km away from us. What will you do if you need help?" asked Luka, worried.

"I am a big girl; I can take care of myself. Besides, I made the best decisions in my life when I listened to my heart. All the trouble started when I lost touch with it. You see, you are already a man, busy with your education, and do not need your mother during the week because you have a place to stay with your employer. We will see each other regularly at the weekends; I will come and visit you."

"Is God talking to you again?" asked Marko, surprised at his mother's sudden change of heart.

"Yes, the famous connection I always told you about seems to be there again. But God is also speaking to you in all possible and imaginable ways. Many people doubt the strength of their personal testimony of faith and underestimate their spiritual abilities because they cannot perceive frequent, surprising or strong messages," Viktoria added.

51

"You mean visions, dreams of revelation or visits from angels? Does God's revelation occur in us ordinary human beings?" asked Luka.

"Like a mother who makes small steps with her little child every day or a teacher who teaches her kindergarten children, God also begins to reveal Himself slowly, patiently and quietly. He leads us through ideas, inspirations, people we meet in life, or the so-called 'inner voice'," Viktoria explains in simple words.

When people say that we should follow our heart or our inner voice, it is because the inner voice is a kind of intuition that we get in touch with when we listen to ourselves. Not only does the Bible tell us of the importance of our heart as a guide, but in Chinese medicine, the heart is considered the master of the body and is responsible for making the final decision about the direction of our actions. When God reveals Himself to man, He does so in a way that corresponds to his condition as a spatial, temporal, individual and social being, consisting of body and mind. The human mind receives its object through the senses; therefore, revelation is communicated to us through images, symbols, parables, similes and allegories.

Paul wrote in the Corinthians: "What no eye has seen, no ear has heard, and what has not entered into the heart of man, that has God prepared for those who love him" (1 Cor 1). Revelation is the fulfilment of the deepest longing, the longing for infinity and fullness, which dwells in man's heart and opens him to a happiness that is not temporary and limited, but eternal" (2 Corinthians).

The great simplicity of the way in which we gradually receive small spiritual clues, which together with time provide the answer we are waiting for or the guidance we need, can lead us to "look beyond the signs."

But how can one trust only small signs and be sure that God is present?

Especially after a particularly difficult phase in life, faith alone is not enough to pull us out of the hole we have fallen into. This is also because when we find ourselves in difficulties, we do not always have the patience or the spiritual keenness to perceive certain signs that let us know that our God is with us. But one thing is difficult to accept today. How is it possible to believe - as it is sometimes said - that God directs history, speaks to people with 'signs,' is present in their lives when all around us evil is growing? If the good God of the Christians really existed, evil would not exist; at least, he would have to intervene to prevent it; if he does not intervene, perhaps it is because he does not exist, some conclude, without considering that everything that makes man suffer is the consequence of wrong use of his freedom; man's wrong choices affect first of all himself and then others, his environment, the relationships that connect him with his fellow men. This is exactly what happened in Viktoria's life, who, in the fever of success, lost touch with herself and with everything that surrounded her. Her illness and the loss of all her possessions made her rediscover her connection with herself and with God.

We must also learn to go beyond ourselves, look into ourselves, and stop blaming God or the system for our disasters. But as frightening as the idea of going on this journey within may be, it is the only way to get to know ourselves and understand what can make us happy, so the first step is to go into resonance with ourselves and bring body, mind and soul into harmony. That body, mind, and soul must be in harmony to live well is surely known to everyone in the advertising spots on the subject of positive thinking. What is now sold as "coaching" was already mentioned in the Bible in ancient times and is still relevant today. This teaches us that the Bible, especially in the books of Proverbs, contains a lot of life advice suitable for non-Christians and non-believers. It is advice that can change your life. Not for nothing is the Bible called one of the most beautiful books for personal growth.

The fact that everything must vibrate at the same frequency to experience harmony, love, success and prosperity is also mentioned in James 1:7: "Do not think that you are receiving anything from the Lord if your mind is wavering and unstable in all your actions."

As we can understand from this verse, the Bible already teaches us that we must be consistent in order to receive something, and above all, how important it is to have the right thoughts is also made clear in a passage in the Letter to the Philippians, in which our heavenly Father teaches us how we can protect ourselves from the attack of our thoughts. In these verses, we also see the ancient form of "mental coaching," which is so popular today.

"Excuse me, but after this revelation from God, did you sell your villa without talking to your children first? But how are you going to live in rent now? You are not used to such a life anymore!" Annika shouted at the other end of the phone.

"Will you stop shouting? That is why I did not say anything to anyone before," Viktoria replied, annoyed.

"Do I understand correctly that this move will only be a temporary solution for you?" Annika asked cautiously.

"That's right, I have other plans that I will reveal in due time."

"But how will you manage all that if you are not always fit?"

"If being fit is the only solution I have left, then I am sure my body will be able to cope with everything. I have to listen to what my heart is telling me. One day, you will understand," replied Viktoria, ending the discussion.

The plan was set: Heart and mind; that is what Viktoria wanted to concentrate on in the future.

Jesus himself, in the decisive moments of his life, including the days of the temptation in the desert, overcame the thoughts and desires "born" in his heart with the Word. To each of the three well-known temptations - the one to turn a stone into bread, the one to commit a spectacular act, and the one to gain the kingdom over the nations by throwing oneself on the ground before Satan - Jesus always replied emphatically: "It is written ...," and thus he "captured" his thoughts in order to subject them to the obedience of the will of God expressed in His Word. David, too, from the depths of his heart, raised this prayer, this lament: "O God, create in me a pure heart" (Psalm 51:10). In other psalms, too, he opens his heart and his mind to the unreserved examination of the Holy

Spirit, of God: "Search me, O Lord, and try me; purify with fire my understanding and my heart" (Psalm 26:2). "Search me, God, and know my heart. Test me and know my thoughts. See if there is not a wicked way in me, and guide me on the everlasting path" (Psalm 139:23-24).

Never before had Viktoria been so sure that the loss of everything she had built up would mean a new beginning for her. Even the illness and the financial disaster had a meaning, even if no one in her family had seen it. While everyone around her saw her as a weak and beaten woman after the storm that had broken over her life, Viktoria saw it all as a new chance for a new beginning that she had given herself. She found herself in much the same position as when she first came to Germany in 1991, except that she was now without a husband and had two sons who were already young men. She had more life experience and was trying to find her way back to God, and she had a different idea of success.

With the certainty that it is not wrong to desire success. God Himself wants us to succeed, and with Jesus's crucifixion, He has provided everything necessary for us to achieve it. If we do not achieve it, the fault lies not with God but with us because we are not persistent enough or too greedy for success.

The greatest mistake we make is to get our priorities wrong and look first for money, then for human relationships, and finally for the Lord. The greatest resource, the greatest wealth we have, is the presence of God and the manifestation of His glory. Nothing is as important as that. God needs people who, like Moses, want to break with the past, with defeats and traditions, because he will work for those who hunger and thirst for him. Let us take the life of Moses as an example for us, for many of us are like him in the same situation. He spent forty years in the desert (Acts 7:30) before he reached the point where God could use him. Awakening often comes out of the desert.

How many people start with nothing and then build an empire? How many people start a business with no initial investment and have great success? How many people have physical disabilities and manage to do amazing things? Do you know what that means? Take the first step, and God will be by your side!

There are times in our life of faith when the Lord speaks in the secret of our hearts, and His voice leads us to develop a relationship with Him. But all too often, we do not respond to God's invitations within us because we do not understand them, and this is where Jesus comes in as if to lead us into the Father's heart, where everything is light. Jesus is the "door" that opens the dialogue with God.

The encounter with Jesus can lead us to the other shore, a different life, and more mature relationships.

Jesus emphasises that he is one of us, like us, with feelings and problems, which makes him accessible to people, especially young people. We all want to be seen as perfect before God because we have the image of the Almighty in us. From Jesus, we have learnt the art of loving without fear and seeing him as one of us. God has done a wonderful act out of love for us, His children, by sending us His Son, Jesus Christ, our brother, to teach us the most beautiful gift we have on this earth: love.

"Jesus, please dry my tears and heal my broken heart," Viktoria said aloud to herself as she sat in the car in the notary's car park.

Even though she had heard God's voice in her heart and was about to go through with her plan to sell her house, Viktoria felt sadness. She was ashamed to turn directly to God and ask Him for comfort. So she turned to Jesus, seeing him as the bearer of her sorrows to God.

In silence, the Word of God can reach the most hidden corners of our hearts. In silence, the Word of God proves effective and sharper than any two-edged sword; it penetrates to the very division of soul and spirit" (Hebrews 4:12). In silence, we cease to hide from God, and the light of Christ can reach us and even heal and transform what we are ashamed of.

How can we explain that ViKtoria followed God's plan blindly, as she had done so many times in her life, but felt ashamed to ask him for comfort? Was it something to do with trust?

Well, she had been through a lot, and she was afraid of making mistakes, afraid, after years of being cut off, that she would not understand and carry out God's messages correctly. Fear. A word she did not know before. What she had gone through, especially during her illness, had left deep marks on her body and soul. She used to do whatever her heart told her without question, but the illness and financial ruin had changed everything. She no longer wanted to make mistakes. She suddenly saw life from a different perspective and evaluated everything at least ten times before she acted. She felt the connection and the need for God but could not let herself fall completely into Him.

To meet God, or rather to be met by Him, means opening oneself to this mysterious dimension we feel in every intense experience. The meaning of a relationship with another person, be it friendship or love, can be found through time spent together, through silence and listening. So it is with our relationship with God. But Viktoria had lost this relationship years ago. There were years in which she could only rely on herself. Years in which she made one mistake after the other. This led her to develop a defensive attitude towards everyone and everything. Sometimes even against herself. Then, there was the view of her friend Annika, who tried to convince her that it was wrong to sell her house and live in a place where she knew no one.

She could no longer keep quiet because God was acting. When we renounce the sounds and voices of the world to remain in His presence, when we do not seek understanding because it is enough for us to be recognised by Him, then silence is faith. Viktoria had allowed herself to be united with God and could not bring herself to fall into His arms.

"I have always loved her house, and I cannot deny that the whole neighbourhood has envied her the good fortune of owning such a beautiful house, which will now belong to me. I can imagine that it is not easy for her to part with such a dream house, especially after all the health problems she has had in the last few years. It would be the same for me. To thank you for choosing me as your buyer and to give you some strength to get through this difficult time, I have brought you a gift," said the buyer after signing the contract and handing her a package.

"It was a coincidence that we talked about this before I could start selling through online platforms. I am happy to know that my house, which now belongs to them, is in good hands. But what have they given me? There was no need to buy me a present," Viktoria asked as she lifted the not-so-light parcel.

"It is an old, well-preserved bible from 1883 that has been in our family for generations. I think it will be in good hands with you."

Enthusiastically, Viktoria unwrapped the Bible and took it in her hands, a beautiful copy with a sturdy dark grey cover and a gold cross in the centre. The very thin pages, inscribed with words she could hardly read in the old German language, gave off an ancient scent. At that moment, she realised she had done the right thing and felt a sense of inner peace.

The buyer for her house had practically fallen into her lap, and she had not even had to look for him. When she had the idea to sell, she had the right buyer, who did not even deviate from her asking price. Was it a coincidence that she had met her neighbour on the street that day and had told him of her intention to sell her house? Was the intention to sell perhaps the trigger for the trial?

Those who believe in God know that it is always up to us to take the first step when we want to achieve something.

Every intention and every wish contains in itself the mechanism of realisation. An infinite power of organisation characterises intention and desire in the realm of pure potentiality. And when we introduce an interaction into the fertile soil of pure potentiality, we cause this power to work for us. Everything in the universe is energy and information, responding to the consciousness that underlies all creation. As explained in the Bible and the books on the Law of Attraction, we attract what vibrates in our frequency through resonance. In order to manifest the desired reality, we have two tools at our disposal: Awareness and Intention. Energy actually follows attention; we energetically nourish what we focus on. Intention, on the other hand, is the engine of desire through which we initiate the energy transformation that manifests the desired reality. We also need three things to achieve our goal: intention, action and belief in success. You may have experienced all kinds of setbacks in your life, but if God has created you for success, your heart will cry out for success, and He will lead you to success.

When Viktoria comes home after selling her house, her children are waiting with their friends and Annika with her husband.
"So? How often did you have to take out the paper towel to dry your tears during the sale?" asked Annika with a hint of sarcasm.
"You mean the happy tears?" asked Viktoria with a grin.
"But tell me, do you still dare to laugh?" irritated Annika asked.
Annika seemed to have a problem with Viktoria's decision, so she took the Bible the buyer had given her out of her pocket and put it carefully on the table.
"When it comes to making decisions, the Bible is a great guide. Did you know that? It can help us gain 'wisdom and understanding' (Proverbs 4:5). In some cases, it tells us what the best decision is; in other cases, it gives us useful advice on how to make wise decisions. Oops... I forgot that you, being a good atheist, probably never had the will or the opportunity to look at this book of wisdom," Viktoria replied.

"Oh, how nice; let me look at the Bible," Luka begged.

"Did you at least sell this beautiful villa for a reasonable price? You know that the economic situation in Germany is disastrous," asked Anton, Annika's husband.

"I told him my price, and he signed the contract without saying a word. It could not have gone better."

"Hippiii, come on, let us celebrate; I have brought a bottle of Prosecco," Marko squealed.

How did Viktoria make the right decisions and make the best of her situation despite the storms in her life and the economic crisis in Germany?

She even managed this, although she still had difficulties connecting with God. The first thing she did was to look at what the Bible says about this. Because our Creator knows what is best for us, His Word contains the wisest advice of all (Psalm 25:12). In some cases, the Bible is clear about what we should do, for example, through laws or commandments (Isaiah 48:17, 18). In many other cases, it is not so specific, but it gives principles that can guide us. These principles help us to make good choices while at the same time leaving room for personal preferences because, as we know, God loves us and always leaves us free to choose. Since she was still having trouble deciphering her heart's messages, and since the Bible tells us that we should not let ourselves be guided by emotions or feelings alone, Viktoria turned to our Lord Jesus Christ in prayer, asking God the Father to give her wisdom. The Bible warns us that we should not always trust our hearts (Proverbs 28:26; Jeremiah 17:9); for example, when we are angry, depressed, discouraged, impatient or tired, we may make unwise decisions (Proverbs 24:10; 29:22). In James 1:5 we can learn that God loves to hear these prayers. He is a caring Father. The Bible says: "God is the giver of wisdom; out of his mouth come knowledge and understanding" (Proverbs 2:6). God gives us wisdom primarily through His written Word, the Bible (2 Timothy 3:16-17).

Sometimes, as with Viktoria, our decision may not please some friends or relatives, but God's decision is wise. There is no reason to worry. Make your choice and stand firm when your heart tells you this is the right choice.

"But what will you do in a new state where you know no one? Here you have us, your office, your clients," Annika insisted.
"You know, in exactly 14 days, I have to hand over the house to the new owner; there is no time left to ask too many questions. I already have all the answers I need and have made my decisions. My office will also be sold, and I will close the estate agency," said Viktoria with the confidence of someone who knows what she is doing.
"Damn it, Viktoria, you have completely lost your mind!" cried Annika.
"Is this your seriousness, mum?" Marko managed to say through clenched teeth.
Everyone in the room looked at Viktoria as if she had come from another planet, while she simply wanted to regain control of her life and reorient herself.

"I have never been so sure that this is the right way. The parade will take place next Saturday; whoever wants to come and help is welcome; I will also have understanding for those who do not come."

These were the few words with which Viktoria explained her position.

"But what will you live on if you give up the estate agency?" insisted Annika.

"Psalm 23... I strongly recommend you to read it," Viktoria advised.

"And you expect me to believe this nonsense after you have decided to lose everything, including us?" Annika shouted.

"Well, if Psalm 23 does not convince you enough, then you can continue with Markus 10, 28-30 .... and we will see each other on the other side of the miracle ..."

Annika angrily took Luka's old Bible out of her hand and quickly searched for the verses from Mark.

Mark 10, 28-30

Then Peter came up and said to him: Behold, we have left everything and are following you! Jesus answered and said; "Truly I say to you, there is no one who has left house or brothers or sisters or father or mother or children or fields for my sake and the gospel's, who will not receive a hundred times as much now in this age, houses and brothers and sisters and mothers and children and fields, with persecutions, and in the age to come, eternal life."

"As I said, you have completely lost your mind!" replied Annika, shaking her head several times as she read the verses.

Chapter 5   Under God's Influence

What is the sky trying to tell me today? Viktoria wondered as she sat on a hill overlooking the whole village. A heart-shaped cloud stood before her in the blue sky. It had been a few weeks since she had moved into a flat in southern Germany, in a village at the foot of the mountains. Almost every day, she went for a walk and saw something heart-shaped, sometimes clouds, sometimes stones, sometimes leaves. And then there were the spectacular sunsets, never seen before, whose colours made the sky glow. She had the feeling of having landed in a place with a completely different energy. Above all, the sight of all this natural beauty moved her to tears. There was such an inner peace in her that she perceived everything around her in a completely new way. Even her attitude to work was different during this time, as if she had taken a break from it. Since her move, she had limited herself to odd jobs that gave her free time; it was as if she was reorienting herself.

What had happened in her life? She still believed in success and prosperity, but she had taken a break from work, taken her foot off the accelerator and reduced herself to a minimalist life.

Was this the influence of God in her life? Was this the life plan laid out for her: to come up empty-handed after the storm that had shattered her life after more than 20 years of devotion in a strange land? Had God really been in control of her life?

Nothing gives us so much strength and security as we understand God's sovereignty in our lives. God's sovereignty is defined as complete, independent and total divine control over every creature, every event and every circumstance at every point in history. Subject to no one, influenced by no one, in absolute independence, God does what He wants, how He wants, and when He wants. God has complete control over every single molecule in the universe at all times, and everything that happens is caused or permitted by Him for His perfect purposes. God has given us the ability to practice faith to have peace and joy and give meaning to life. In order for faith to unfold its power, however, it must be founded on something. There is no more solid foundation than faith in our heavenly Father's love for us, his plan of happiness, and Jesus Christ's ability and willingness to fulfil all his promises. For some, faith is something incomprehensible and is therefore not fully utilised. Some think that the guidance that can be received through firm faith is not rational. But faith is not an illusion or magic but a power rooted in eternal principles.

Only those who have faith know that they can achieve everything in life if they follow God's principles;

We must believe in God and his will to help us in our need, no matter how difficult the situation may be.

To obey his commandments and to live in such a way that he can trust us.

To be sensitive to the silent inspirations of the Holy Spirit.

To be courageous in following these inspirations.

We must be patient and understanding when God makes us struggle to grow and when the answers come gradually over a long period of time because a motivating faith is based on trust in the Lord and his willingness to respond to our needs.

"Why do we hear so little from you since you moved? Now that you have more time, you have no time to call me..." complained Annika on the other end of the phone.

"You know, since I am here, I have developed an incredible inner peace. I do not know when I have ever felt like this before, just being alone in nature and being moved to tears by a sunset. I do not even know how long it has been since I took the time to do nothing," replied Viktoria with a serenity that was not of this world.

"But how can you do nothing all day? You need a job, you need to interact with other people, you need to go out with men, and, of course, you need to have sex. Have you forgotten that everything around you is life?" cried Annika.

"No, I have not forgotten, but you see that I have lost the connection to myself through all this doing, and now I feel the need to do nothing. My heart tells me so."

"Are you aware of the change you have made? It is almost impossible for the people around you to understand what is happening to you. And then your tattoo, how could you come up with the idea of having the name of 'Jesus' tattooed on your skin? Have you lost your mind?" Annika asked.

"I do not know if I would have been able to come closer to God and achieve this positive change for myself without Jesus' intervention in my life. My children also notice that I am more relaxed. Also, I have not planned to be without a job or to remain single all the time, which will change when the time is right. In your eyes, everything I do seems wrong. You know that I am old enough, right?"

"I have the impression that you are possessed by a sect that is ruining your life..."

"Tell me, are you crazy? Who the hell told you that Jesus Christ is a cult? Probably the devil himself, I would say ...," Viktoria commented sharply and ended the conversation.
As much as Viktoria loved her friend, Annika, she could see that their differences of opinion were becoming more insurmountable as time passed. While Viktoria respected her atheist beliefs, Annika took every opportunity to criticise her and her love of God. It seemed as if her best friend had turned against her just because she had decided to live her life differently and to find what was hidden deep inside her. She had embarked on a completely new way of life, which meant a profound change and a complete departure from old habits.

Slightly annoyed by Annika's behaviour and accusations, Viktoria prayed to Jesus in silence: May He ask His Almighty Father to give her the wisdom to understand what gift He has in store for her on this new path of life.

I ask You for the grace to continue on the path You have shown me. Guide my Lord Jesus Christ in all my actions and decisions. I am exhausted after all that I have gone through, but I trust in You that I will be regenerated physically and spiritually to receive the strength to continue on this new life path.

'Do you aspire to the greater gifts? I will show you a better way. 1Co 14:12'.

The more regular her connection with Jesus became, the more Viktoria felt that the messages coming from her heart were clear, and her inner peace grew. She felt understood by Jesus. She felt his closeness as if she had a friend beside her who knew exactly what she was going through. Do you know why?

Jesus cried

Jesus was rejected

Jesus was ridiculed

Jesus was wounded

Jesus was betrayed

Jesus was tempted

Jesus was abandoned

Jesus is one of us! And like us, he has felt all the pain of freeing us from sin.

In his righteousness and goodness, the Lord will show the way to sinners of all times and places. He accompanies us lovingly on our difficult journey, which demands humility and fear of God. But his omnipresent help does not seem to be enough. What do we lack? Or rather, what do we need to give up in order to walk the path of righteousness and justice?

To learn the way God proposes, we must free ourselves from our deepest convictions, hostility, malice, fears and worries, and above all, we must learn to love, love ourselves and be happy. Then we will be able to open ourselves to others, to forgive ourselves and to forgive others; we will discover how precious moments can be in which we pause, sit down, become silent, listen to the things created by God, and be close to them and to listen to their voice. On the path the Lord teaches us to walk, we can rediscover love and the desire to be part of a community; we discover the beauty of brotherhood and sisterhood in Christ. Prayer is a fundamental element for our social and spiritual growth. In prayer, we place ourselves before God and recognize him; we can more easily enter into a relationship with ourselves and with one another. United in prayer, we can be close to one another, be reconciled and feel united in Christ.

In her search for a new path, Viktoria began to rediscover what it was like to work for others after having been her own employer for ten years. Suddenly, she felt drawn to the catering industry and convinced that this would be a way of earning money and getting back in touch with civilisation. So, she started looking for part-time jobs at all the local restaurants. Just like when she first arrived in Germany in 1991, she was able to find a job four times a week, which enabled her to pay her way and get out of the house.

"You come across as a real industry expert," her employer told her at the end of the first day's work.

"I am very happy about that. Thank you for allowing me to try out this new field," she replied shyly.

But at the end of the day, she realised that, although she had never worked in the catering industry before, it was easy for her to do the job as if she had always done it, just like when she came to Germany in the nineties and started working immediately without knowing the language.

Somehow happy to be back at the top of the success ladder, Viktoria called her children to get their opinions.

"This may sound disappointing, but I have started a job in the catering industry today," Viktoria said as her children listened to her over the speakerphone. "Are you listening to me?" she asked when there was no reply.

"Wow, respect, that is really impressive," Luka commented.

"Absolutely. I think so, too. And how does it feel?" asked Marko.

"Well, I have to say, I like it!" she answered in a funny way, and all three of them burst out laughing. "You find it funny?" she asked as the boys continued to laugh.

"Do you work for an Italian?" asked Luka.

"Sure, who else!"

"Be careful, you know that Italians have a reputation for being womanisers," said Marko.

"Is that so? I thought that all men in general were womanisers..."

"It's nice to hear that you are doing so well, Mum?" said Luka.

"I thought I had disappointed you with my expectations, having been reduced from an independent manager to a waiter in a 'Womanisers club'."

"If you think we see you as degraded because of this, you are wrong. In our eyes, you have not lost your dignity just because you work for others. We know very well what you are capable of when you rise to the highest level. For the moment, we can say that all three of us are on the same level and that you, like us, are at the beginning of your future career," Marko told his mother proudly.

With tears in her eyes, Viktoria asked softly, "Where do these beautiful words come from?"

"From the heart," the boys replied at the same time.

What a joy for Viktoria to hear such words and to know that her family was united.

God seemed to be influencing not only her but also her boys in a positive way, for all three seemed to be on the same wavelength. Viktoria has always had a special bond with her children. From birth, her children were accustomed to hearing about her faith in God. In keeping with the family tradition, Viktoria had also had them baptised in a Catholic church and taken to their first communion. Before she officially left the Catholic Church, she taught her children with a group of other children who were to go to First Communion in the same church. She was the only mother in the group to offer catechism classes. It was a wonderful experience for the children and her, especially because she could teach only what she thought was useful and not the standard curriculum of the Catholic Church.

As her children grew up, Viktoria continued to pray for the little everyday things in their lives: Friendships, sports, health, school exams - because, as we all know, the Lord invites us to take all our cares to Him. But as she read and studied the prayers of Paul for the people she loved, she also realised the fundamental importance of prayer for the spiritual needs of her children. On some days, especially after she had started her own business, Viktoria tended to forget prayer because of the hustle and bustle of life. However, she knew that her children's greatest need was not momentary happiness but growing holiness. Holiness and happiness are not contradictory but intimately linked. Holiness leads to true happiness: the everlasting joy of a soul rooted in Christ. When she asked God to make her children holy, she prayed for their highest good. From childhood, she had programmed her children for happiness, prosperity and success. Paul's prayer for the Philippians helped her understand how to pray for the sanctification of her children.

I pray that your love may become richer and deeper and that you may gain more and more insight and understanding. In this way, you will learn to decide how to live so that on the day when Jesus Christ will sit in judgment, you will be able to appear before your Judge without guilt or sin. All the good that Christ creates in a guilt-free life will be found in you. And all this to the glory of God and his praise! Philippians 1:9-11.

Praying for the success of her children's careers was also part of Viktoria's ritual of accompanying, motivating and supporting them in their careers - at least until the time when she and Ivan began to struggle for a higher income. She ultimately lost touch with herself and with God.

One of her favourite prayers for success, which she also taught her children, was this;

"Lord, guide my actions, watch over my tongue, bless my efforts, guide my decisions, and help me be the best I can be so that I can honour Your name in my life and career. I pray for success, God!"

Many will be surprised to hear the phrase 'guard my tongue'. Well, even the Bible emphasises the importance of controlling your tongue, as the current Modern Coaching Programme recommends.
'Death and life are in the power of the tongue; whoever loves it will eat its fruit. Proverbs 13:3.'

Words have power: They can decide between life and death. Those who like to hear themselves talk must live with the consequences.
What comes out of the mouth reveals what is in the heart.
The Bible has much to say about using the tongue, the lips, the mouth, words and language. God created man in his own image. He gave man the ability to speak and communicate and express himself in words and sentences. When God gave people this ability, He also gave them a part of His authority and creativity. Indeed, the Word of God created all that is alive. (Psalm 33:6; Hebrews 11:3). The power of the Word greatly influences our behaviour. It is therefore good to take this subject very seriously.

Modern coaching programmes tell us that talking about life goals with other people can affect our motivation and brain anatomy and prevent us from achieving our goals. But why?

It is normal that we feel the urge to talk to others about the plans we have in mind and that self-disclosure (or sharing valuable information about ourselves) helps to create intimacy in relationships. Before we do this, however, we should consider certain situations.

To achieve a goal, it is important to have the conviction that this goal can be achieved. Some people are absolutely sure of what they want to do, but others have doubts and fears and are not so sure. If we share our goals with others before we reach them, we risk receiving all kinds of opinions and advice, and many of them will probably not be encouraging. Those close to us may be pessimistic about our project, constantly pointing out what can go wrong and encouraging us to give up. Even if they do not mean any harm, their comments can make us doubt, hesitate and even build up a mental wall that limits us considerably.

Even as a child, Viktoria noticed that the inner voice within her was calling for success while the people around her were trying to tell her that it was not possible, especially for a woman, to achieve what she wanted.

Viktoria had the strength to ignore this and later realised that the limits others tried to set for her were her own. Unfortunately, as we all know, it is not always easy to think rationally in such situations, and one tends to develop doubts and fears and give up one's dreams as a result. Viktoria had the courage to ask for prosperity; she had the patience, and everything in her life ran smoothly until she and Ivan started competing.

The ability to wait and be patient is also mentioned in the Bible in several chapters. What we learn through patience will strengthen our character, raise our lives to a higher level and increase our happiness.

'A patient man is better than a strong man, and he who keeps his peace is the winner of cities. Proverbs 16:32'.

But if we have faith and live under the influence of God, why do we tend to be untempered again and again?

Quite simply, we live in a time when we can no longer wait and must have everything under control and quickly. In the age of speed and "here and now," waiting is one of the most unpleasant conditions. Not everyone understands that waiting does not mean not to move but to move better because even a seemingly tedious waiting can lead to useful considerations for our improvement. We experience changes so quickly that we do not even have time to analyse them, and already we are beyond them. This happens every day. We have no time to go to the cinema to see the latest episode because another one has begun, the song that one could not miss last month is forgotten today, and we have a new one. It is the same when we leave the small and enter the macro: the job market, communication, relationships, and all the areas in which we are able to live are changing so quickly that it leaves us speechless. We experience changes so quickly that we do not even have time to analyse them, and already we are beyond them. This is what happens every day.

Before her illness, Viktoria was also in a frenetic rhythm, where she and her now ex-husband Ivan played the game of who had the most and who earned the most, forgetting the main reason that had brought them together to start a family: love. But her body eventually forced Viktoria to slow down first and then stop.

It was only when she moved to a new city that she began a new era full of life and success plans, with a clear head and the confidence that she had the Lord on her side. Trusting in the support of her Lord Jesus Christ and the voice of her heart, which showed her the way, she assessed for the first time in years all the possibilities for solid and lasting success.

"Good evening, Viktoria. You look good today," said her boss, Gianni, as she entered the restaurant.

"I'm married," she replied with a lie to get him off her back.

"Oh, that makes no difference; I am not jealous," he confirmed with a wink.

"Well, it's going to start, just like my children said," she thought...

The first challenges of the new career had begun. In all her years as an employee in Germany, she had never encountered a womaniser as an employer. Nevertheless, she seemed to have patience with Gianni's extravagant behaviour; it seemed as if nothing could take away the serenity she had found.

Sometimes, maintaining inner peace can seem like a full-time job, especially when we have lost it for so long. We need peace in our circumstances, peace in our relationships and peace with God. To remain constantly in peace and serenity does indeed require a great deal of determination, but it is possible to achieve it. Psalm 91:1 says: "Whoever dwells in the protection of the Highest shall rest in the shadow of the Almighty." Being Christ teaches us that prayer is the first step in finding peace. We must never cease to trust in God, for He has the last word in every situation. Go with confidence and firm hope towards Jesus and his promises because the way with him is the secret of triumph and happiness. There is no other way.

If we look at the first part of Psalm 37, which explains how one can have peace in God even in the midst of difficult situations, we will see that this Psalm reminds us that the life of a true Christian is a journey of faith. It is a journey on which we must direct our gaze to what we do not see and not to what we do see. For if we focus our gaze on what is visible around us, on the injustices, the difficulties, the things that are going wrong, then it will be impossible to live a life of joy; rather, we will have a life full of sorrows, burdens and a troubled heart.

When you have the presence of Jesus in your life, you will experience the holy order of God. You will have peace and tranquillity; you will not feel anxiety or fear and will not have to run. Progress in your spiritual life is not achieved when you have enjoyed the grace of consolation, but when you have remained steadfast in faith with humility, self-denial, and patience, you are convinced that all things will turn out for your good. For by grace, life is full of blessings. It is important that we recognise the blessings in our lives and thank them! But it is also true that life is full of difficulties and trials while we are here on earth!

Chapter 6 A special will

Should I get married? What career should I choose? Should I move to a different house or city?

Doubts overtake us when we are faced with important decisions, and nothing comforts us more than the certainty that we are at the centre of God's will in the decisions we have to make. Yes, but what is God's will for us in the decision we have to make?

And if there is a certain will of God for the decision before us, does this mean that we have erred, that we have misunderstood God's perfect will and that we will live the rest of our lives outside the blessing that He has intended for us?

It seems strange that so much doubt and uncertainty can arise from such a pure and saintly desire to bring our decisions into harmony with the will of the Father.

One stands at a crossroads, has two paths before one and does not know where to go. Perhaps you ask God for a clear sign, as you did with Abraham, Gideon or Paul. One thing that can very easily happen is that we concentrate so much on trying to understand God's special will for our life in a particular situation that we forget what God himself has already so clearly revealed to us through His Word.

"Finally you come to visit us after all this time, but what have you been doing all these weeks on your own?" asked Annika when Viktoria reappeared.

"Nothing special; I spent a lot of time with myself."

"And just to be alone a little, you had to move so far away? We miss you so much," Annika explained.

"I miss you too, but this way I am going now is something very special for me; I have never felt so much gratitude for my life and love for myself as in the last weeks."

"But gratitude for what? You have lost everything, and you feel thankful?" Annika inquired.

"Grateful for what I have found again. Myself."

"Well, finding yourself could have happened to us."

"You have to come and visit me so that you understand what I mean. You know, since I have been living in Germany, I have never been to a place where Jesus Christ is constantly present. There are beautiful crucifixes at the entrance and exit of towns, and when you drive along the highways, you see crucifixes in the middle of the woods or in the mountains. All this gives me the feeling of being on the right path. And it is not just the presence of crosses or crucifixes; I feel his presence in me, and my life changes in a positive way...."

"Mmhh, let me think for a moment... I see no change except that you have landed at the bottom of the world...," Annika said calmly.

"Discussing with you is a waste of time," Viktoria confirmed, shaking her head.

After Viktoria tried to overcome defeat and focus on the essentials by looking at the world with new eyes, she came up against Annika's superficiality. In a period of reflection on the many beautiful things in life, in which she learnt to appreciate the invisible with a new perspective of gratitude and joy in the small things, she slowly felt the urge to distance herself from her best friend, Annika. After dinner, she retired to her guest room, lay down on her bed, opened her Bible, closed her eyes and prayed;

"My merciful Jesus Christ, please give me a sign that I may understand if I am on the right path."

'Truly, truly, I tell you: He that believeth in Me, the works that I do shall he also do; and greater works than these shall he do; for I go to the Father. John 14:12'

'Mmhh, ok....that is also a very meaningful instruction,' Viktoria thought and wondered, but does that only apply to men or also to women?

This verse is a hymn to belonging. In a society where the tendency is to isolate oneself, remain distant, and not get involved, the foundation that Jesus offers us is exactly the opposite of all this. It is the feeling of intimacy with him. It is participation in everything he does, with the potential of our inner hunger. The words of Jesus are full of this thirst. They are the song, the poetry of the Gospel.

For Jesus, it does not matter whether we are great but whether we have understood how to do great things. Faith in him is essential. To believe is to be consecrated to him, to become like him. To do his works with the same passion is to live according to his received and believed teachings, like the vines that grow from the union with the vine. When Jesus chose the twelve disciples, he did not do so because he needed partners, collaborators, secretaries...

Jesus chose them so that they would be with him (Mk 3:14). Because he needs friends with whom he can share his life, his way, his mission, to whom he can pass on the juice of grace. As far as friendship is concerned, the situation between Viktoria and Annika was not exactly exemplary, especially after Viktoria's decision to move to another city to be closer to God. However, as she read through the book, she noticed that some of the sayings and psalms were dedicated to women.

'God is in her midst; she will not be shaken; God will help her in the morning. Psalm 46:5'

Although the Old and New Testaments are written in the masculine form, we find many female figures. We must not forget that woman is the first witness of Jesus' resurrection, the foundation of Christian doctrine, and the first true evangelise. The disciples of Jesus have healed women, also free women, because they have been "liberated" not only from evil, from the devil or from sickness, but also from social oppression, from a structure that relegated them to a secondary position and sent them home in a state of submission. With this liberation, the dignity of succession was given to them. Some of them, like Tamar and Ruth, dared to break the laws of men to defend women's rights. They make courageous choices but are also defended and accepted by God. Alongside them are theologians who have read the sacred texts differently and transmitted a different version. The alleged inferiority of women, which results from the interpretation of certain biblical passages, has served, above all, to legitimise the discrimination and subordination of women, but it is not obvious that this is the true and only meaning.

'Strength and dignity are her dress, and she laughs at the coming day. She opens her mouth with wisdom, and there is kind advice on her tongue. Proverbs 31:25.'

When Viktoria read this, she burst into tears. What wonderful words, what wonderful plans! How beautiful it is to see how God loves to explain the sense of things in His 'wonderful' plans to His children and people who are close to Him. The more she read in the Bible, the less the shipwreck seemed like a defeat. In the last few weeks, she had stopped feeling sorry for herself, and unlike Annika, she no longer thought about what she had lost. Although her friend's behaviour irritated her, she tried to maintain her mental integrity. A slight smile curled around her lips, and she said to herself, "He who does not fall is sitting. He who does not fall has not tried. I am quite different from the way some people see me, and I am glad that I fell, but above all that, I got up again."

It is almost normal for people to feel ashamed of their failures, and they ignore the fact that failure is an essential part of life for everyone who is not so stupid as not to admit or recognise it. Failure is feared more than anything else because it means having failed in the eyes of others. Those who feel that they have failed are weighed down by a burden that they often feel is unjust and undeserved and from which they are unlikely to emerge unscathed. But when Viktoria reflects on her experiences, on the poverty she cannot be proud of, even in retrospect. But when

Viktoria reflects on her experiences, on the poverty she cannot be proud of, on the fear of disappointing those who have greater expectations of her than she does, like her children, to whom she wants to be a great role model, then she realises that she has to learn the most important lesson of all. The lesson that no university in the world counts among its subjects, and for which there is not a single exam to be passed but a constant, daily test that will accompany her for the rest of her life. The power of the will on a difficult, complicated and uncontrollable path brings her closer to God.

With the Bible in her hand, Viktoria fell asleep peacefully. She did not yet understand what God was doing with her, but she felt His presence in everything she did.

"Come on, get up, you sleepyhead; it is already ten!" called Annika from behind the door.

"Ohh shit!" replied Viktoria, still sleepy.

"I thought we were going on a trip today; look how nice the weather is," said Annika, who came into the room and was already pulling up the blinds.

"I have completely lost track of time," said Viktoria.

"Judging by the position of the pages, you must have done a lot of reading last night ...," Annika said, pointing to the still-open Bible.

"Yes, that is true. I think I reached a higher level of wisdom while reading."

"Come, let us go and have some breakfast, Miss Know-it-all ...," Annika said with a hearty laugh.

In the meantime, Viktoria no longer paid attention to Annika's attempts to avoid the subject of faith and everything connected with it. She was not interested in what others thought about it but only in what she felt. Annika associated happiness with other things or experiences. She could see nothing positive in what had happened to Viktoria; on the contrary, she found every opportunity to emphasise the severity of the experience and to criticise Viktoria's reaction to it.

"What do you think is the secret of happiness?" asked Annika at breakfast.

Viktoria choked up when she heard this profound question from her friend Annika.

"Well, if I were to answer you in my own way, I would know that this beautiful, sunny day would end in a storm...," Viktoria said, raising her eyebrows.

"I know that we disagree for various reasons, but a few days ago, I read something in a magazine that made me think a lot," Annika said seriously.

"Does it have anything to do with believing in God and Jesus Christ?"

"Well, I believe that the world makes us live in a great delusion, which is the root of all unhappiness, all failure, all defeat, all sadness or depression. The world makes us believe that we must do what we want in order to be happy. They tell us not only that God does not exist but also that if he does, he is boring and wants us to limit ourselves to following his laws," Annika said calmly.

"Hearing that from you is quite impressive. Does that mean you believe in God now? The point is that God exists and that His laws are ways of love, not meant to lock us in a cage but to give us complete freedom and joy. If a river had no banks, it could not reach the sea; it could not fulfil its function as a river; it would not fulfil what it was created for. So it is with man."

"Have you now found your destiny, the destiny your God has planned for you?" asked Annika curiously.

Annika's curiosity, which sees no immediate results in Viktoria's life, shows us that it is not always easy for the people around us to understand the reasons for our decisions, especially our chosen path. Self-discovery consists of recognising one's own desires and authentic principles within oneself, free from the influences and expectations of society, friends and parents, which sometimes, even with the best intentions, can lead us astray or distract us from our own path. Each person has his or her own talents, characteristics, desires, dreams and values that make him or her unique. If a person pays attention to his or her uniqueness and consciously searches for what distinguishes him or her from others, he or she will recognise within himself or herself what he or she needs to do or leave out in order to be happy. In other words, he or she will feel compelled or 'called' to certain decisions and behaviours. Regarding vocation, some people start a career at a very young age and stay in the same job for thirty years. Others experiment here and there, find their calling in adulthood, and then experience a cascade of success and prosperity.

But what is vocation, and what does God have to do with it?

Well, vocation is the plan God has designed for each of us to carry out. It is only in our relationship with God that we can discover it, for it depends to a large extent on him who reveals it to us, first through the call, which is his initiative, and then by providing us with the gifts to fulfil the specific task which he entrusts to us. All that is left to us is the response, which depends entirely on our freedom and generosity. Vocation is often manifested in SIGNIFICANTS, which need to be heard and interpreted.

We can see vocation as a combination of different elements: We love the object of our vocation, and we love to engage with it. In this sense, vocation overlaps with passion. Whatever we do out of vocation, we do it very well, whether it is painting, riding or playing sport, we have an innate talent for the activity in question and, last but not least, the result of what we do interests someone else who is also prepared to pay for it.

When we read some important pages of the New and Old Testaments, we notice that at the beginning of every true vocation is the Lord, who chooses and invites us to follow him. He is the one who calls, and this is indeed the deepest meaning of the word "vocation," which means "call." In the Gospels, we often see Jesus calling those whom he would later make his disciples. The initiative comes from the Master, and the vocation is a gift of grace, just as our Lord Jesus Christ makes us a good and fruitful earth. So, our success is God's will. Every vocation is personal and carries within it a unique key, like a password known only to the one who receives it, and it unfolds in a specific time and context, writing a personal history made up of special and significant moments. Gifts, personal abilities, and potentials are all the gifts that God gives to the person called out of love to enable him to love in the right way and to respond fully to the call he has received. These gifts can be of a physical, spiritual, moral or spiritual nature. They affect all areas of the person and must grow and mature with time. Our Father sent Jesus to help us fulfil our longing and the love written in our hearts. The Holy Spirit gives life to this desire, preserves it and brings it to its full development. The Son Jesus Christ, sent by the Father, gives a spiritual form to every experience of love. Then we can say: The Lord has chosen us, and the Lord guides us. The Gospel tells us: "I have chosen you out of the world." This knowledge must be constantly present in us and always ring out when the separation from the world challenges us. The Lord has chosen us, the Lord guides our steps, and we only need to pray for clarity and wisdom.

Prayer so that God may reveal His will to us is the first step we must take if we do not know His will for us. Prayer requires a militant attitude; it is not for wimps because, with prayer, we are clearly oriented towards God because prayer is part of the order of love, prayer is passion, and yes, prayer is already in us! Yes, prayer is already in us! The Lord reveals to us where it is hidden: "It is not in heaven that you speak: Who will go up in heaven for us, to fetch it for us and bring it to our ears, so that we may do it? It is not on the other side of the sea that you say: Who will drive for us over the sea, fetch it for us and let us hear it so that we can do it? On the contrary, this word is very close to you; it is in your mouth and heart, so you may put it into practice." Deuteronomy 30:12-13.

But what are the signs of vocation, and how do we recognise the will of God?

The best way to avoid wasting years or decades of life and to act effectively is to explore oneself and understand the right path for us. In fact, finding one's vocation means taking a series of precise steps to learn to listen to an inner voice amidst the noise of the constant external constraints that characterise our society. Normally, we try to understand the signs that can point us in a direction, the path of life that God has marked out for each one of us. The signs of a vocation are many and varied and can appear in different ways. Intuition and spiritual sensitivity are a good example. One feels an ever-increasing awareness of wanting to be with God, seeking his presence and meditating on his Word. It is also a burden to see the needs of those who suffer without being able to help in any way. In other words, there is more than personal ambition and the desire to save souls, show mercy to others, and use one's life for what one is called to do. Then, in addition to the will to succeed, you have a passion for helping others, and the needs of the weak and suffering are at the centre of your thoughts. In your daily life, you are generous to your fellow men. You feel ready and compassionate towards others, you feel that the love that unites you with God makes you somehow more open to others, and you know that if you are successful and even make a lot of money, you will also do good to others.

For Viktoria, once she had survived the storm, the most important thing in understanding her vocation was to find out where to start, analysing her life to understand which aspects were better and which were worse. Money? Her relationships? How was her physical and mental health? How nice was her day? How much time did you spend on activities that were not productive but which cleared your mind and relaxed you? These are simple but necessary questions.

Since the spiritual person also succeeds in attracting and receiving what he desires, living in harmony and in love with Jesus is the key to success in work, social relationships and love. Jesus himself has given us this overwhelming revelation: "If anyone loves me, he will keep my word; and my Father will love him, and we will come to him and make our home with him" (John 14:23). The discovery of one's vocation and of God's will for us requires, above all, the ability to enter deeply into one's own interior dimension, to grasp the messages that he is constantly sending us and to recognise the role that Jesus plays for us in God's plan, because, as Jesus says to Thomas in John 14:6;

"I am the way, the truth and the life; no one comes to the Father except through me."

Invite Jesus into your heart to become your personal Lord and Saviour. Accept Jesus Christ as your Lord and Saviour and follow God's plan for your life, as written in the Bible. Make Jesus your personal Helper because when you have found your calling, it does not mean it is all downhill from now on. Life will always present you with challenges that you must face, but if you do so knowing that your being on earth is for a purpose, it will give you unparalleled strength and a sense of wholeness. If you have not yet concluded or understood what your vocation is, then know that you do not have to go far, for it is buried in your inner garden, the golden seed. It is your vocation, the task to which you feel called, the life task for which you were born. It is a seed because it lies within you in a potential form, and in order to grow, it needs your care; it is golden because it is of inestimable value, and to recognise and nurture it means to transform your own being, for you will become what you think you are, and the vocation is already within you!

"Have you also discovered God's will for you, yes or no?" asked Annika when she got no answer from Viktoria.
"Why do you care? You don't believe in God…"

Chapter 7   Accepting God

"I and the Father are one," Jesus whispered to ViKtoria in her dream.

She woke up one Sunday morning, shaken and in tears, and sat on her bed for a long time. For the first time in her life, she had dreamed of Jesus. To dream of Jesus at such a delicate time in her life was a moment of great comfort and protection, a sign of God's presence in her life. But as she sat on her bed, still a little dreamy, the insistent ringing of her mobile brought her back to reality.

"Mum, I have to tell you something strange that happened to Luka and me this morning," Marko said at the other end of the line.

"What happened? Why are you so upset, and where is your brother?" she asked in horror.

"We're going to church," Marko replied.

"What, you are going to church? What have you done that you have to go to church at this time?" she asked, confused.

"Nothing. We got up very early this morning, and both of us had this urge. And what are you doing?"

"Oh, that all sounds very exciting. Sitting on the bed, I woke up after a conversation with Jesus."

"A talk with Jesus? Did you perhaps drink alcohol last night with your Womanisers employer?"

"Mhmm, no, I did not. Besides, I left the Womanisersclub yesterday..."

"Really? Don't tell me that the Womaniser dared to stretch out his hands..."

"Well, he was a bit rude, and I left without comment. When I got home, I did a quick Google search for restaurants, and lo and behold, I got a job at a German restaurant run by a mother and daughter. They are very nice people. The owner is terminally ill."

"Are you going to move from restaurant to restaurant until you retire?" asked Marko worriedly.

"No, I have other plans..."

"Oh well, then I am reassured. But tell me about your dream with Jesus..."

"First, tell me about your desire to go to church..."

How did it happen that Viktoria and her children, all three at the same time, felt a kind of spiritual vocation?

The spiritual change that had taken place seemed to extend to her family, but it did not seem to extend to the professional change for which Viktoria felt no urgency. Had Viktoria lost the will to succeed? Was she no longer interested in success and wealth? When Viktoria least expected it, she began to melt again in the presence of Jesus Christ, who seemed to embrace her whole family. Her priorities had changed since her illness and the loss of her possessions. What she had experienced made her realise that success presupposes a good relationship with God, a connection with herself, health and a healthy family. The idea of success on its own, as pure success for the satisfaction of the ego, seemed to have disappeared from her mind. All these years, she had shown what she was capable of when she wanted to, but her success had developed in an unhealthy way. Not only did she recognise that a change was necessary, but she also felt that this change was a necessity for her.

We often find it hard to understand something simple: Our lives are full of change. Perhaps it used to be easier to have a deep dialogue with God through intense daily prayer. Perhaps now we need a different kind of prayer because something has changed in us. When we accept change, we better understand ourselves and the world around us. And what is this change?

It can mean many things: that we have lost hope in a certain project, that we have fallen into a routine for some reason (this does not mean that our whole life is a routine; it can also be just one of many aspects of our daily life), that the people around us have finally infected us with their thoughts, that experiences and attitudes - for various reasons - have changed into something else (some see the world differently now, others are not as close to us as before), that we have simply become more mature, for example. The possibilities are endless! God is still there and ready to listen to us.

For Viktoria, this dark period of her life was not a negative but a positive time because it is precisely when one is tragic that one can recognise that there is a God and that one longs for a relationship with Him. Sometimes, feeling God a little more is necessary when you have been used to understanding Him for a long time. In solitude, Viktoria learned to listen to the silence, recognise herself, and open her heart to Jesus. As so many who have had similar experiences say, the desert, the darkest time of life, is the very place of encounter with God. There are things of which we know: that the grace of God is not exhausted and that God has chosen us as we are. He chooses us even if our steps are small, fickle and fragile. And it is in these small steps that he waits for his kingdom to become a reality. He wants life, hope, joy and light to triumph. We are chosen by him to be witnesses of his light, freedom, and presence and to understand that the light we seek is ourselves. To be chosen by God is always an expression of love. One knows that one is called, chosen, and wanted, and everything around one changes. Life has a meaning. There may be a time when we understand less, and our hearts are touched more. But discovering what has changed is the beginning of a new stage in our relationship with God.

If God wants us to dare something, let us be encouraged by his presence. Have I not told you? Be courageous and undaunted; do not be afraid or frightened, for the Lord, your God, is with you wherever you go" (Joshua 1:9). Cast all your cares on him, for he cares for you" (Peter 5:7). Trust the Lord with all your heart and do not trust your mind. Remember him in all your ways, and he will make your paths right" (Proverbs 3:5-6).

"But how come you changed jobs again? You have just worked for five weeks with the Italian, and then you move to another place? To a place where you get less money! But how is this regression possible? What is wrong with you, Viktoria? We are really worried about you!" shouted Annika on the other end of the line.

"What's wrong with you? I'm fine, I'm not starving, I'm fine. Did it ever occur to you that I make my life a little uncomfortable, that

I leave my comfort zone to learn things I had forgotten, and yes, to awaken the warrior in me?" asked Viktoria calmly.

"Do you not see that you are regressing? You were made to be a successful woman, and now you are wasting your time and talent in a restaurant for a pittance, and the crazy thing is that you are happy doing it. You say you are following a certain direction that your heart or Jesus has given you, and you are falling deeper and deeper. Don't you think it's time to get professional help, I mean a psychologist?" said Annika, almost scornful.

"Instead of going to a psychologist, I think it is time to end this friendship because you obviously do not understand what I am trying to do!"

"Viktoria!!!! Damn it!" Those were the last words she heard as she ended the conversation with Annika.

During this conversation, Viktoria wanted to take the opportunity to tell Annika that she was in Switzerland to set up a new property company, but her friend Annika only saw the negative in Viktoria's life, whereas she had never felt as balanced as she did at this time. During her illness, she had always been able to count on Annika's support, but not now, in a time of change, especially after she had decided to change her life. Annika did not understand that Vikroria had not given up on success but was striving for a healthy and lasting success that God blessed. 'For whom the Lord blesses, he will bless; but whom he curses, he will curse. Psalm 37:22.'

God will bless us!

We must understand that God wants us to be blessed! We must anchor this in our heads and hearts because God wishes that it goes well for us every day of our lives on this earth. There are so many promises in God's Word that we should be blessed. No one says this; the Bible and God say this. As long as the earth stands, it shall be sown and reaped, and it shall not cease (Genésis 8:22); there shall be an abundance for all, and this applies to everyone who believes! The same seed has a natural power and the power to multiply. When a seed is sown, it will bear one fruit and many! This applies to everything we sow in our lives, and we sow well. If we live according to God's principles, we will always be victorious. Even in stormy times, we remain stable because we receive God's peace and always trust Him. God wants stable people in his kingdom, not emotionally moved people. What do you do when things are not going well? Do you despair, or do you continue to trust in God? If you want to see what is inside an orange, squeeze it. Think of Paul and Silas - they were in prison when the disaster came, but they praised God; think of Stephanus - when he was stoned, he saw the heavens open and the throne of God; they were truly men of God. Recognize people of faith in times of crisis, for you show who you are in times of crisis.

Ask God for help! The time will come when God will wipe away all tears; He has seen your tears, but first, He has seen your faith - and God answers faith. Viktoria had no doubts about this, which is why she stood by her decisions, whether her best friend Annika or the people around her thought she was a failure. God wants you to be blessed in everything, including financial matters. There should be nothing lacking in your home; yes, you should be so blessed that you can bless others with it. God blesses all our paths when we choose to walk them; he blesses not only our perseverance but also our weakness. When David ascended the throne of Israel, he said: "I am still weak today, though I have been anointed to be king" (Samuel 3:39). The moment we put our faith in Jesus, God saves us with the Holy Spirit. However weak or inadequate we may feel, God, like David, can use us in extraordinary ways. Even our weakness is blessed. Our weakness is also blessed.

"You know, Viktoria, I do not know how long I have to live, but my daughter and I are very happy to have you in our team. Our customers are delighted with your friendliness and your work. God bless you," the new employer said to Viktoria at the end of the evening.

"God bless you and your family, and may you have many happy days ahead of you," replied Viktoria, her heart full of gratitude. She felt at ease and knew that her decision to move had been the right one.

It was amazing how her motto had changed in the last few months from "Work hard and you will succeed" to "Work hard on yourself, and with God's help, you will succeed."

Viktoria's most valuable work? Working on yourself.

If you want to grow and improve your life, you must be willing to accept change, the Bible tells us. The Gospel of Luke proclaims the message of a compassionate God and encourages us to learn from God and to dare his freedom and greatness. So often, we cherish the dream, the illusion of a life without worries, without limits, without prohibitions and without having to bear the burden of others.

Life is change; change is life. Standstill is death.

What the grub calls the end of the world, the rest of the world calls a butterfly. What the foetus calls death, the rest of the world calls birth. What you call the end is the true rebirth.

The Gospel invites us to change constantly: nothing can be stopped. Those who do not change will die.

Today, I am not wearing yesterday's shirt (hopefully!); today, I do not have the same hair as five years ago; today, I do not have the same friends as ten years ago; today, the people I live with are not the same as twenty years ago, and so on. Everything is changing. Everything is changing. In twenty-two days, our skin cells change; in three months, all the cells of our body change. Every three months, we are different; we change. But how many of us have a fear of change: 'Oh no!'

Think of the relationship of a couple: How many changes there are! But will we be able to manage them? Do we have the will? Will we accept the challenge of change? Or will we say "Oh, no" each time?

We must go from being lovers to being companions: Can we accept that the "butterflies in our stomach" become love and passion but also mature and mature? Or do I want to be the centre of the other?

Partners become parents: Can we accept that we are no longer the only recipients of our partner's love but that this love is shared with our children? Or do we become competitors? Or will we only take care of the children and forget ourselves and our partner? Or will we be lonely?

As adults, we will experience how our children grow up, leave us and become older. Will we be able to change and move from doing to being, from external to internal design? Or will we lose ourselves in doing and find no meaning in our lives?

It is normal that we have fear when we are confronted with change, especially big changes. Who is forcing us? But life is change, development, becoming. Not even the dead remain the same! Let alone the living!

These were the insights that Viktoria gained the moment she let God into her life, things that Annika, as an atheist, could not understand, all of which caused their friendship to break down.

"One of our clients left this note for you; he wants to sell his house. We told him that you were an excellent agent. He also finds you very handsome...," the employer told Viktoria.

"You've found me clients in the property business?" asked Viktoria, surprised.

"You know, one can see that you can do more than just serve food and make drinks. I am old, and I do not have long to live; I know all kinds of people, and I know who is talented and who is not. I do not know what has happened to you in your life, and I do not want to interfere with your private life, but I am sure that you are a very talented woman. You radiate success. Since you have been here, our restaurant has blossomed; you have taken care of the smallest details, and you have put flowers and candles on the tables. You could have done without, but you take the time for the little things."

"I am not trying to run away from success, but I need different experiences. I love the property market, but I needed a break. I am sure it will be good for me to get reacquainted with your client's property, and, to be honest, I am glad to be doing it. Thank you for the recommendation."

Without Viktoria having looked for work, work suddenly started looking for her. It was a completely new situation that she had not reckoned with. Even the people around her began to see her differently. How was this possible? It was almost as if the others could see the light coming from her. As she invited Jesus into her life as Lord and Saviour, Viktoria experienced more and more true peace and freedom. She felt awake and radiant, filled with the Holy Spirit and with the power to lead a new life, as it is written in John 1:12. Jesus is the only one who can set me free, as it is written: "If the Son makes you free, you are truly free" (John 8:36). If we entrust our lives to him and let him be our Lord, then much will happen, the impossible will become possible.

Grateful and touched at the same time, Viktoria fought back tears, shut herself in the toilet for a moment and prayed in silence: "I entrust myself to you with all my heart and soul, Lord Jesus Christ. I open to You the deepest and most hidden places of my heart.

Jesus, you are the Lord of my whole life; I believe in you and accept you as my Lord and Saviour.

When all are asleep, God is at work; when all is dark, God shines; when all seems impossible, God is at work in silence: This is the mystery that never ceases to fascinate and shake the conscience, that raises questions in search of credible explanations, that challenges naïve faith and presumptuous rationalism.

"A light shines in the night, and the people who walk in darkness see it" (Isaiah 9:1). An extraordinary paradox: when one walks in the dark, one can see the light. We all know this: To walk at night is terrifying, to stay awake at night is exhausting, to resist fatigue is difficult, and to sleep is easier. But to sleep is to give up! Make peace with God; He will lead you to the light. Do not be ashamed, and do not be too proud to pray! Let God inspire you because when God inspires us, we must take the initiative; we must become active and not remain passive and immobile. In order to understand God's grace given through Jesus Christ, our Lord, one must ask in faith. Pray! Ask God to help you get back on your feet, ask God for health, ask God to bless your beautiful family and give you prosperity. Ask for success! Rise up and shine, look, your light; the glory of the Lord is upon you. Turn your eyes and look; let your heart beat with joy!

Radiant in an elegant white shirt, skirt and pumps, Viktoria stands in front of the house of her first real estate client. Her black leather bag with pen and notes still smelled like new. Half-closed, she held the leather bag to her nose several times. "God, how I have missed this," she thought to herself.

"Mrs Moravec, right? I hope I pronounced your name correctly," said the attractive man with the southern features.

She nodded her head with a smile, without being able to say a word, and thought: "Oh, what a male beauty...."

"My name is Wolf, Robert Wolf. Would you like to take a look inside?" he asked.

"Of course, yes. It is a beautiful house and still quite new, as you can see from the outside. I don't want to be too intrusive, but why are you selling it?" she dared to ask.

"Divorce..." he replied.

"I'm sorry," she said sympathetically.

"You must not be sad; not everything bad happens by itself. Besides, I would never have met her if I had not offered the house for sale."

Slightly red in the face at the compliment she had just received, she asked him: "Aren't you sad about the sale?"

"It's only a house. Everything can be rebuilt if you believe in it," he replied.

"Good attitude," she replied.

After a long period of solitude, Viktoria felt a little nervous at the proximity of a handsome man.

"Tell me, do you live in this area with your family?" he asked firmly.

"How much do you want to sell the house for?" she asked, changing the subject.

"You're not wearing a wedding ring," he added.

"How many square metres is the house?"

"May I invite you to dinner?" he asked cheekily.

"I've only known you for a few minutes, and I can already imagine the reason for your divorce..."

"What do you mean by that?" he asked, amused.

"That I have to store your data under 'very demanding customer'," she replied and tried to leave.

"Let's start with the house, even if you don't want to have dinner with me..."

"Great, I thought I had come for nothing..."

This is great... The more faithful I am to His will, the more the Lord gives me new opportunities to grow," she thought, as she found herself in one of the most exciting situations since she had been alone.

She had a somewhat turbulent start to prove herself once again, but perhaps this was exactly what the Lord had in mind for her. After all, this client had practically fallen from the sky. Was it God's will to put her in uncomfortable situations? In 1 Corinthians 10:13, we read: "For no one has ever tempted you except a man, but God is faithful and will not overstrain you, but will also give you a way out of the temptation." This verse teaches us a wonderful principle. If we belong to it, God will not allow any difficulty that arises in our lives to be too great for us to bear. In every temptation, in every trial that comes our way, God will remain faithful and show us a way to overcome the trial.

Who has ever learned anything from comfortable situations? You do not learn from comfort; you do not learn from easy situations, accept the trials of life, smile at the pain and accept it. Difficult moments and pain are the prelude to success. The pain is asking you: "Do you want to achieve your goals, or are you just a chatterbox?" And no matter where you want to go, pain is the one that paves the way to the top. It is only in pain that we recognise that it is time to change something in our lives, and above all, we recognise Jesus. He does not leave us to suffer; he suffers with us; he walks with us in suffering. It is only through pain and suffering that we can really know him and perceive his presence. If we entrust ourselves completely to Jesus, suffering can become an opportunity to experience a piece of heaven on earth, for in pain, our true Christian vocation shows itself. How is it possible to have joy in the heart when pain pierces it? Because joy is hidden in pain.

"When should I bring the clients for a visit?" asked Viktoria, having noted down all the information necessary for marketing.
"Now, immediately?" he asked.
"First, you must sign the broker's contract; only then can I begin with the marketing..."
"My pen is ready," he replied with a twinkle in his eye.
"You must give me a few days; then I will send you the contract."

As she left the house, she felt warmth on her face, a kind of overwhelming feeling of joy. She felt she had made a good impression on the seller.

"There is never a second chance to make a good first impression," she recalled Oscar Wilde's famous words.

There had been a lot of water under the bridge since the presence of a man had alarmed her. Quickly, she glanced at the house and saw that he was watching her from the window.

"My God, please give me the wisdom to understand whether this is an attempt or a new possibility," she prayed on her way home until the ringing of her mobile interrupted her.

"Are you married? If you won't go out to dinner with me, then at least tell me if you are married," the male voice asked.

"You seem to be in real pain," she replied and hung up.

Chapter 8 A profound change

"What? You started a property company in Switzerland?" asked Luka.

"Yes, exactly. I went to Switzerland this morning and set up a company. I am planning to move to Switzerland in the next few months and have already got a lot of things underway," replied Viktoria.

"That sounds completely crazy. But if I may be honest, I think it is great. You see, Mum, our training is in danger here in Germany because of the ongoing economic crisis. Our boss told us today that since the war in Ukraine and the Corona pandemic, everything is very difficult. He also fears that the war could spread to the whole of Europe. There is even talk of reintroducing military service. This scares us because we are both at an age when we could be sent to the front."

"Concentrate on Jesus, not on the storm, says Matthew 14-22,33; I do not know how many times I have repeated this verse in dark times. Do not let bad thoughts overwhelm you; Jesus is working in our family. How long can you stay in training?"

"Now your friend Annika would say: Oh yes, Jesus is working in your family by not preventing your two children from losing their apprenticeship? Well, our boss has filed for bankruptcy. But tell me, I thought you no longer wanted to be self-employed, and now you even set up a company in Switzerland. How is that possible?" asked Luka in surprise.

"Well, you know that our Lord Jesus Christ would never do anything that could harm you, and the loss of the apprenticeship will certainly have a different meaning. Because of Switzerland, I believe that God simply placed this dream in my heart when I almost had no courage left to be independent, as if He had chosen me for something greater. Obviously, I have been equipped with the right tools. Otherwise, He would not have let me dream of something so big. Maybe I am the one in the family who will break the cycle of poverty. I hope so."

But despite their confidence in God's plans, doors suddenly closed for Viktoria's children. A new challenge seemed to have entered Viktoria's life just as she had begun to rebuild. Was she waiting for the next test? Had she taken the step to Switzerland at the right time? Had she set her sights too high again?

'Lord, teach me that my life has a purpose. Psalm 39:5.'
To achieve a goal, one must submit to God. The Bible says in James 4:15-16.
Even though Viktoria did not see immediate success in her life, her life seemed to improve day by day since she had come closer to God through Jesus Christ. Her physical well-being and inner peace had improved. She had stopped asking so many questions and worrying so much about problems and had experienced that solutions often came of themselves without her having to force them or worry about them.
This may not seem obvious in the midst of a challenge, but it is an undeniable truth.
However serious or daunting a challenge may seem, it is important to remember that it will not last forever. Every storm passes, every night gives way to a new day, and every problem

finds a solution. In the midst of difficulties, it is easy to lose sight of this reality and to think that our struggle is endless. But this is not so because the Lord is always with us.

God gives us countless opportunities to return to Him and to experience His love anew. Our God is the God of the second, third, fourth and many other possibilities. He does not only give us a 'second life,' but he comes to us to change our whole life.

'Fear not, for I am with you; be not dismayed, for I am your God. I will strengthen you, I will help you, I will guard you with my victorious hand. Jesaja 41:10.'

Fear of failure can be described as the paralysis of action that nips projects in the bud, makes us recoil at the first obstacle, and leads us to abandon them because the fear of failure, at least apparently, outweighs the possibility of success. Fear blocks, paralyses. It is not for nothing that the most frequently quoted word in the Bible is "fear not," for the Bible also says that fear is a natural and often justified feeling. Fear of God, for example, is seen as a good thing because it reminds us of His power and our place in the universe. But the Bible also encourages us not to be afraid of what makes us afraid because God has promised to protect us and give us the strength to face our fears, and the Holy Spirit frees us from fear and makes us feel the love of God.

Through him, fears are overcome, and doors are opened. For this is what the Spirit does: He makes us feel God's closeness, and so his love dispels fear and illuminates the way.

So take all your fears to your Lord Jesus Christ so that you may open your heart to God and accept Him through the transformation; pray that you may be helped to find the way that leads you to God; do it in simple words, you do not need to tell a novel, but whatever you say, say it from your heart and in faith;

"Spirit of the Lord, come down on me, melt me, form me, fill me with yourself, fill me, use me, heal me."

Only when one accepts God can one understand the true meaning of faith and apply it in all matters of life, including the search for new professional opportunities, love, health and, of course, success, where faith, perseverance and patience are emphasised as decisive elements for success.

In Matthew 6:25-34, the Lord lists ten reasons why Christians should not be anxious and worried, which, if followed, will free us not only from all forms of anxiety but also from the resulting diseases that afflict our bodies and which modern medicine calls "stress diseases."

The Christ, who has already accepted God and recognised the transformation, avoids fears and worries because he knows:

Life is more than food (v. 25);

The body is more than clothes (v. 25);

People are more important than birds (v. 26);

God cares for both (v. 26);

Fear is useless and ridiculous (v. 27);

Man is superior to plants (v. 28);

God adorns like no other (v. 28);

Whoever worries is like a pagan (v. 29-32);
He who worries is an unbeliever (v. 32);

We live from day to day (v. 34).

The end of a challenge may not be obvious, but knowing it is a beacon of hope in the darkest moments.
It is this knowledge that allows us to persevere, to continue, to fight on. However difficult the challenge may be, it is only temporary. In these moments, it is important to have confidence and to carry on and make a breakthrough. Put everything in God's hands and avoid forcing situations. In addition to His abundant and effective grace, the Lord has given you the mind, the hands and the spiritual gifts to make your talents bear fruit. God is constantly working miracles - raising the dead, making the deaf hear, making the blind see, making the lame walk... He has shown us all this through His Son, Jesus Christ. Your talents, your aspirations, your successes - they are worth nothing if you do not give them to Jesus Christ if you do not make them available to him, if you make them a god. You alone with your boat, if you renounce the Master, you are sailing, supernaturally speaking, straight into shipwreck. Only if you seek the presence and guidance of the Lord will you be safe from the storms and waves

of life. Put everything in God's hands: Your thoughts, the beautiful adventures of your imagination, your noble human ambitions, and your pure loves must pass through the Heart of Jesus Christ. Otherwise, sooner or later, they will go down with your selfishness.

If you want to have a contented heart, if you want to feel true joy in your heart, then you need two things or rather two aspects of the same thing: You have to acknowledge Jesus Christ as your Lord and Saviour, and in order to really acknowledge Jesus Christ as your Lord and Saviour, you have to acknowledge Jesus Christ as your treasure, and you also have to continue to grow in Jesus Christ so that you can accept God.

When we work on our spiritual transformation, we are transforming our hearts into a greater love for our Creator and the creation. We take time to listen to God's message in creation 'with awe and wonder.' We reflect on our words and actions, humbly acknowledge where we have failed, and practise new ways of living simply and in solidarity with creation. By transforming our hearts and minds to a greater love for God, our fellow human beings and the creation, we set in motion a process of healing and renewal in our homes, our lives, our families and our communities. When the Bible speaks of repentance to God, it usually refers to a profound inner change that grounds and motivates a transformation of life.

In the call to repentance, we can see the whole of biblical faith. The divine word is intended to bring about repentance in its hearers. The word testified to in the Holy Scriptures will promote that existential movement back to the dream of God that is made possible by a different view of life in the world. The whole Bible speaks of repentance, not just where the Word appears. The whole of existence is a process of conversion that cannot be reduced to a single moment, however decisive it may seem to us. In the biographies of human beings, there are indeed defining, shattering experiences, but the biblical logic of conversion makes these luminous moments the beginning of a lifelong journey.

"Mrs Moravec, this is Robert Wolf, do you remember? You have been instructed to sell my house. Your brokerage contract arrived today, but on the letterhead under your name is a Swiss address. Have you moved?"

"I am just about to move, but you need not worry about the sale of your house; I will do everything as we agreed."

"Will you have dinner with me before you move?"

"You are very persistent! I am still considering it...," Viktoria replied, this time not even reluctantly.

"Are you religious?" he asked suddenly.

"That is a very interesting question. And you, are you religious?" she asked back.

"Do you find the question interesting? I believe in God. And you?" he simply replied.

"I do, too," she replied, pleased.

Is it not interesting that a man of God is interested in Viktoria and that he is interested in her in a rather insistent way? Since Viktoria had accepted God into her life and was, above all, God-fearing, her plans for the future in terms of love and a future marriage should also correspond to her faith plan. Not only should

113

Viktoria's future professional and personal success be built on a solid and healthy foundation, but also the love for which she had asked God, should there be a next man in her life, that she should experience the highest essence of pure feelings that one can have for a partner.

But is it God who brings "love" together?

Those who know God know that He directs man's steps in a mysterious way, but not at man's expense or "by magic," for "grace requires nature."

This little sentence says a lot about how God's grace, his providence and his plan are realised and materialised. To speak of the meeting of two people in love is to speak of the meeting of two freedoms, two openings or even two closures! The encounter between two people is not only about God's will, which must be carefully discerned and not projected, but also about the freedom of two people, their history, their desires and their wounds. In addition to these freedoms, in reality, there are all sorts of other freedoms and situations that help or hinder encounters. Rather than "waiting for the gift of heaven," as it is said, it is wise to do one's part, to be open to encounter, to confrontation, without haste, but also without fear.

There is a beautiful phrase in the Bible in which the angel Raphael says to Tobias (referring to Sarah): "Do not be afraid, she is destined for you from eternity" (Tob 6:16-18).

The encounter with this man, who not only wanted to enable her to do business but also took an interest in her and was a man of

God, was interpreted by ViKtoria as a sign of God's direct intervention in her life. Will this unlikely encounter change the course of her life and open unexpected doors?

"The same God who gave me the idea for the business will also bring me the customers. And maybe even love?", she thinks to herself.

Viktoria not only had to start from scratch, but she also needed time to heal her heart, so she focused on her relationship with Jesus Christ, the one man who had managed to gain a place in her heart and since Jesus was sent to unite those whose hearts were broken, he was now the most important point of reference in her life, because the heart of Christian life is Jesus Christ.

In reading the Bible, it is important to look for Christ. In the Old Testament, we can see many types of Christ: People, events, or things that represent Christ and his work in some way. There are also many prophecies about Christ.
Let us take, for example, Isaiah 61, which, more than any other prophet, was led by the Spirit of Christ to describe things and aspects of Christ.
In chapter 61, there is a prophecy that Jesus referred to himself when he read in the synagogue of Nazareth. Although these words were written by Isaiah, they belong to Jesus Christ. It was the Spirit of Jesus Himself that caused Jesaja to write these words;

1 The Spirit of the Lord, God, is upon me; for the Lord has anointed me to bring good tidings to the humble; he has sent me

to bind up those whose hearts are broken, to proclaim liberty to the slaves and the opening of the prison to the captives, 2 to proclaim the Lord's year of grace and the day of our God's vengeance, to comfort all who are afflicted.

Jesus applies this passage from Isaiah to himself. They are also the words of Jesus Christ, which He announced through the prophet Jesaja some 600 years before His coming into the world.

Let us recall the first part of Isaiah 61:1;

"The Spirit of the Lord God is upon me; for the Lord has sent me to bring good news to the afflicted" (Jesaja 61:1).
The Spirit of the Lord God rests upon me.
When Jesus was on earth, the Holy Spirit was on him.
When Jesus Christ was baptised in the Jordan by John the Baptist, the Holy Spirit descended from heaven and came upon him, as we read in Matthew 3.

"And when Jesus was baptised, he went up out of the water, and behold, the heavens were opened upon him, and he saw the Spirit of God descending like a dove and coming upon him; and behold, a voice from heaven said: This is my beloved Son, in whom I am well pleased" (Matthew 3:16-17).
In the Bible, the Holy Spirit has descended on different people and enabled them to do certain things. But He always came in a limited way. On Jesus, however, the Holy Spirit came without limits, as we read in John 3:34.

"Whom God sends, he speaks God's word; for God does not give the Spirit according to measure. (John 3,34).
The Father gave Jesus the Spirit without measure, without limit.

Jesus was also anointed, as the scripture says:

"The Spirit of the Lord is upon me, for the Lord has anointed me to bring good news to the humble" (Isaiah 61:1).
Jesus was anointed. To be anointed by the Holy Spirit is to be called to a ministry.

"But who are you, the nice, friendly waitress from the old restaurant around the corner or the confident businesswoman who sold me the house at the first viewing? Who are you, Viktoria?" asked Mr Wolf.
"I'm probably a mixture of both," Viktoria grinned.
"Do you know what the disadvantage of this quick sale is?"
"That you now have to say goodbye to your beautiful home even more quickly?" asked Viktoria, confused.
"I had already said goodbye to my house. Well, I had hoped that I would see you more often because of the customer appointments since you do not want to go out to dinner with me ... Will we see each other next time at the notary?"
"Yes."
"May I at least invite you to our Free Christian Community on Sunday?" he asked hopefully.
"A Christian church? I did not know that there was such a thing here. I wanted to find one for a long time," she said euphorically.
"Now it seems like I hit the right button..."

"Yes, you have..."

With an indescribable feeling, Viktoria left the house and went to the car. The thought of Jesus and attending a Christian church filled her heart, and it was as if her chest exploded with love. It was as if the love from the heart of Jesus was setting her heart on fire. Viktoria had experienced such a feeling as a young girl, but not as intensely as the present perception of this conscious love for Jesus.

"I love you, Jesus," she repeated in her mind as she sat in the car, putting her hand on her heart and imagining Jesus coming towards her, embracing her and telling her that he loved her. Jesus Christ was leading her to the healing process as the love of Jesus was penetrating her more and more. In her thoughts, Jesus embraced her and made her feel important. He healed the bleeding wound in her heart. Jesus did not come to erase the pain she was feeling but to heal the wound that the pain had caused. In other words, The painful memory does not disappear from the subconscious of the mind, but through prayer, it is transformed into a positive memory by the presence of Jesus.

He lovingly leads the wounded girl Viktoria to entrust her pain to God, her Father.

But how was this possible?

"Whoever joins himself to the Lord becomes one spirit with him (...) Do you not know that your body is a temple of the Holy Spirit who is in you and whom you have received from God? Therefore, you do not belong to yourselves, for you were purchased at a high price. Therefore glorify God in your body" (1 Cor 6:17-19).

More and more, the meaning of the verses she was reading in the Bible became clear to her.

Jesus said: "I in them, and they in me, and I will ask the Father, and he will give you another Comforter to be with you forever, the Spirit of Truth, whom the world cannot receive because it does not see or know him. But you know him because he lives in you and will be in you" (John 14:16-18). This is wonderful! "When the Holy Spirit comes, you will know that I am in the Father and you are in me" (John 14:20). This is not just a connection, but a unity. This is God's goal, his dream of love, his kingdom: "I in you and you in me." When the Holy Spirit works in us, it is accomplished. Then, our spirit, our body, our soul, and our mind become God's dwelling place through His Spirit! Every cell belongs to Him, every breath, every heartbeat, every moment. The work of the Holy Spirit is to consecrate us, to transform us, to bring about a kind of transubstantiation in us, and then we are all of Him, and He is all of us.

"Mum, we are coming to visit you on Friday and will stay until Sunday. What do you think about that?" asked Marko.

"I think you would make me very happy. Have you talked to your boss about the training places?" asked Viktoria.

"Yes, and you will not believe what happened. Did you know that this company also has a branch in Switzerland, which does very good business? He offered us two apprenticeships there," Marko said enthusiastically.

"Really?" asked Viktoria excitedly.

"Yes, really. Don't you think that it's a happy coincidence that you've just started a company in Switzerland?"

"It's more than a coincidence, and it's a real miracle, I would say!"

"You know, that is exactly what I was thinking. I wonder what your friend Annika would say..."

"I think she would find something negative in all the positive. She saw my fall as something terrible and not as a new opportunity. While for Annika, the fall meant the end, I came to prove that the fall would be the door to a new beginning. That we lost everything here was probably the preparation for the next step," explains Viktoria.

"My brother and I want to discover Switzerland, and we are looking forward to it," says Marko.

"Let's go this new way..."

The encounter with Jesus Christ changed Viktoria from within, and everything around her seemed to respond to this change as if God was using her obedient will to bless others.

The Bible says that a time will come when the true servants of God will serve in spirit and in truth, and that time has come. More and more people are turning to Jesus. We will use our bodies and our voices to pray because praying does not stop when the music stops; praying is a way of life; it is your way of life! You show whether you are a believer, even outside the Church, by your lifestyle, by your actions.

What does that mean? That what God has said to you is true in your heart and that you really believe in the Word of God.

The Word of God speaks to the heart more than 100 times; prayer begins in the heart. But when I say heart, what do you think of it? The muscle in your body? When the Scriptures speak of the heart, they mean the character, the mind, the thoughts, the conscience, the feelings and the will. In reality, the heart is something like a command centre that can control feelings, emotions, character and will. There is always someone who sits in this command centre: That is where God should be.

Viktoria came to the Free Christian Church with her children at an early age. Being there moved her so much that she could hardly hold back her tears. The melodious guitar music during the rehearsal before the service made her shudder.
A light illuminated the writing on the wall;

"I am the way and the truth and the life; no one comes to the Father but through me" (John 14:6).

 "Mum, here, take this handkerchief," said Luka, who handed her a handkerchief to dry her tears.

Just before the service began, Viktoria looked around for Mr Wolf, who had invited her and seemed to have forgotten about her. But she could not find him anywhere.
A young woman went to the piano and sat down with an open book of music. A young man began to play the guitar, and when the door behind the speaker's podium opened, everyone began to sing.

"Peace be with you, dear brothers and sisters," greeted Mr Wolf from behind the lectern.

Chapter 9   Jesus is your breakthrough

"Yes!!! We got the contracts for the new training places in Zurich!" Luka rejoiced as they ate lunch in the restaurant.

The loss of the apprenticeship was not a loss but an impulse for the next step... The beautiful verse from Jesaja 60:22 comes to mind: "When the time is ripe, I, the Lord, will make it happen...," Viktoria answered happily.

Within a few weeks, the lives of Viktoria and her children were swept away by an unstoppable current that took them out of Germany as if the time had come for an outbreak!

Full of trust in the Lord, Viktoria decided that it was time to look at apartments in Switzerland and gave notice to the landlord. She had exactly eight weeks to move to Switzerland while her children stayed with her employer in Zurich.

With her hands on her heart, Viktoria held back her tears of joy; her voice could not speak, and her heart screamed with gratitude. Untiringly, she looked at God's creation in her life, a creation that was so amazing, so colourful, so beautiful, comparable to the trees that are bare in winter, while the earth is still wrapped in its white winter coat, and a thin layer of snow covers the ground. Time seemed to stand still, to be suspended, and then, quite unexpectedly, life broke forth; life triumphed!

"You have turned my mourning into dancing; you have stripped off my mourning and girded me with joy. Psalm 30:12."

Have you ever let Jesus into your life? Jesus comes into your house and puts everything in order!

Like Viktoria, you will never be the same again after your encounter with Jesus. When you call on Him, He enters your heart spiritually and takes away your sins through the power of His sacrifice. Jesus gives your life a new value by helping you to remove the thoughts, feelings and behaviours that prevent you from living your life in harmony with God. If you need a breakthrough, it can only come through the Messiah. Jesus is your breakthrough, and you can have a breakthrough in any situation you are in. Let Him be your personal breaker, and the breakthrough will come.

The Bible paints a realistic picture of life: Blessings and sorrows, mourning and dancing, grief and joy. This is life. No gloom and doom, no rose-tinted glasses. Joy and sorrow - both are part of life. Otherwise, life would be either terrible or terribly boring. And it is only against the background of pain and suffering that we can experience joy and happiness as something special: Nothing is self-evident, least of all that we are well.

Jesus is the fundamental discovery that can give a decisive turn and meaning to our lives. He is the hidden treasure, the precious pearl of which the Bible speaks. It is also a matter of searching, of breaking forth and of striving. Let your heart burn with longing for the precious treasure that is Jesus.

The word of Jesus Christ calls you today to look at his mercy. It calls you to see how he, the good shepherd, comes to seek you, to bring you healing, to give you healing.

Perhaps right now, you are a lost sheep. Perhaps you have sinned, perhaps life has wounded you, perhaps you have experienced a dramatic moment. Now, Jesus Christ is coming to you to bring you out of the darkness, out of the darkness that you have fallen into. The important thing is that you are not afraid. Sometimes, when we are wounded, we let fear overwhelm us. That is exactly what the devil wants: to make you afraid, to depress you, to discourage you. Maybe you are even getting used to your servitude. But none of this comes from God. Jesus will bring you out of your inner death. Jesus Christ is not angry with your sins. You may be the worst person in the world today, the most disgusting person on earth, but Jesus Christ is not angry with you because He is waiting for you with open arms to save you! He does not want you to be lost because He has redeemed you with the blood of His Cross!

"The guy who bought your house brought me a letter for you today, apparently from Switzerland," Annika said in a rather conservative tone.

"Nice to hear from you; I hope you and your family are doing well," Viktoria replied, surprised to hear from her friend Annika.

"Yes, we are fine, thank you. But what does this letter from Switzerland mean? It seems to be from the authorities. What are you up to, Viktoria?" asks Annika in an admonishing tone.

"What am I up to? Nothing you would understand," answers Viktoria.

"Damn you, Viktoria!" shouts Annika.

"Be good, Annika, please send the letter to my address in Germany."

It was a few but clear words that Viktoria found for her friend Annika. Words of a person who is not influenced by the opinions of others and who walks in God.

Have you ever said in your life: "I never thought this would happen; it really is a miracle! If so, then you know that this is the effect that Jesus has on your life when you stop and see how He has changed it for you. How much truer and happier it is now! And how different it is now to look at the same life that you may have felt was your last! How could this miracle happen? Through the grace that the Lord gives to those who turn to him with trust. For how many things can you thank the Lord for today?" asked Mr Wolf during the Sunday reading.

For Viktoria, who had experienced several miracles in her personal life in recent weeks, these words were confirmation that what she was experiencing was the hand of the Lord in her life. Physically and mentally, she felt different, too, a well-being that she no longer knew when she had experienced it for the last time. In spite of the hardships she had endured during her illness, she felt that she was living in a new, more vibrant and resilient body. The body that had been disfigured by the many operations became for her a perfect body, a perfect body because God created it in His own image.

"You seem to feel comfortable in our Christian community," said Mr Wolf to Viktoria after the service.

"I feel at home everywhere lately," she replied with a smile.

"Yes, and you can see it; you radiate a light that does not seem to be of this world...."

"Strange, but everyone says that to me," she says, aware that her inner change is also visible on the outside.

"In three days, I have an appointment with the notary for the sale of my house, after which I would like to invite you to lunch at the restaurant where you sometimes work," Mr Wolf went on the attack again...

"Yes, OK. Why not?" she replied this time.

He looked at her incredulously and asked: "Really?"

"Yes."

"I just wanted to tell you that I recommended you because of the excellent job you did selling my house. I have a friend who has an architecture firm here in town, and he is looking for someone to do some sales projects, and I am sure that you are the right person for the job," he added.

Surprised, she looked at him silently for a moment and just said: "God bless you."

Was that the plan God had for her? Was this the reason why the system of her old life had collapsed and she had lost everything? Did God have something better in mind for her?

The pursuit of heavenly wealth through prayer for financial wisdom is an important reminder that all our resources ultimately belong to God and that He has commissioned us to be wise with them. As we focus on God's will and seek His guidance, He will give us the wisdom and strength to make wise financial decisions. We can be sure that God will never let us down and that He wants us to be successful in all areas of our lives. But what do we gain by investing in Jesus Christ?

Anyone who knows anything about finance would say: If you want to make money, you have to invest, not just a little and with little risk, but you have to invest a lot and risk enough to increase your profit. Otherwise, he will always remain poor. But Jesus tells us in Luke 17:7-10 that only the one who invests his whole life, only the one who puts his whole self on the line, can receive the kingdom of God. This requires the courage to take risks, not someone who sits back and waits to see what happens.

In the parable, it is not success that is rewarded but the willingness to take risks. It shows that small faith and unbelief are punished. There is a promise in faith, or to put it in the language of finance: Faith brings profit; it brings return.

Where, then, does the material blessing come from? The Bible says in 5. Deuteronomy 8:18;

"Remember the Lord, your God, for he will give you the strength to gain wealth."

If we put God first, He will take care of all our needs. The Bible says in Matthew 6:33: "Seek ye first the kingdom of God, and his righteousness, and all things shall be added unto you."

It was exactly according to this principle that Viktoria's life seemed to go up again after she had realised that everything is only possible when you put God first. This also shows that God

has not forgotten us and that the miracle, the breakthrough, the healing, the long-awaited door to finally open is coming to us.
A fulfilled life comes only from joy and from contact with the Word of God.

The Word of God helps us, nourishes our inner man, and gives us comfort and perspective. We can confess with the prophet Jeremiah: "Your word is my food, whenever I receive it; your word is the joy and comfort of my heart" (Jeremiah 15:16).

The Word of God was suddenly so clear in ViKtoria's life that she felt she could only go up from here. As she sat in the waiting room of the architects' office, she silently thanked the Lord for the opportunity to lead a project of this magnitude. But that was not her only thought. The notary appointment an hour later was also on her mind. But not the one with the notary, but the lunch with the attractive, divorced Mr Wolf.

"Mrs Moravec, right?" the architect asked, shaking her hand.

"Yes, right. Thank you for inviting me here today," she replied, pleased that she had won a new client who had practically fallen from the sky.

"Thank you for being here. Mr Wolf told me how competently and quickly you sold his house. People like you are rare in these times," the architect praised.
"Let's see, the notary appointment with Mr Wolf is in an hour."

After a discussion about marketing a property with six units already in the planning stage and two future new-build projects with four units each, Viktoria left the architect's office in order to market the first six units immediately. Her commission for the first project was in the five-figure range. Tears of joy streamed down her face. For a long time, God had been silent in her life, but suddenly, it seemed as if he had come out of his silence.

Anyone who reads the Bible knows that there are many places in Scripture where people have to endure God's silence. People who waited years for a child (Abraham and Sarah, Samuel's mother Hannah, and the parents of John the Baptist, to name but a few). The whole people of Israel lived in slavery in Egypt for hundreds of years (!) until God heard their cries. Elijah had to wander 40 days in the desert until he found God and found him in the silence. The Pharisees of the New Testament waited with longing and sincerity for the Messiah but could not see him in Jesus because he did not meet their expectations.

Many cannot accept God's silence because they do not understand the meaning of silence; man has always looked for answers to the difficulties and catastrophes that afflict humanity.
Sacred Scripture also speaks of God's silence towards those who pray. In this respect, the silent God is the culmination of a journey of suffering. The believer, faced with difficulties, implores God, as the Psalms say: "God, do not be silent"; "God of my praise, do not be silent! (Ps 83:2); "When you are silent, I am like one who descends into the pit." Jesus himself turned to the Father at the extreme moment of the cross: "My God, my God, why have you

forsaken me?" These are the words of Psalm 22 that follow: "My God, day and night I cry out to you for help, but you do not hear me and give me no rest."

Are we the ones who cannot hear and understand God's silence? Are we the ones who do not understand that the divine word is expressed in unexpected events? God speaks in silence. It is also silence and word: "When a deep silence surrounded all things ... your all-powerful word came from the royal throne."

The Bible also tells of other apparitions, often linked to the history of Israel. God appears to the people in light, in darkness, in silence. God appeared to Moses on Mount Sinai, and when the mountain shook violently, he responded with lightning and thunder. After the last gasp of Jesus on the cross, God speaks. Again, with an earthquake that shatters the veil of the temple, shakes the earth and breaks the rocks. The divine words spoken in silence can be understood through the beauty of the Creator's design.

Nor is the problem a God who seems distant and silent, as if he had erected a wall between himself and the faithful, but the lack of listening to man, the longing for an answer that corresponds to "our image and parable." This is where our faith comes in and our patience in waiting for him to do what he wants to do in order to achieve the best that he has planned for us.

"Here, dry your tears and fix your make-up. Otherwise, the notary might ask you some funny questions," says Mr Wolf in the car park outside the notary's office.
"These are happy tears..."

"I heard you signed the contract with the architect; congratulations," he said, obviously happy for you.

"I owe all this to you. May the Lord bless you abundantly."

"Oh, I think he already does," he said, looking deep into her eyes, causing her to cringe.

The turning point in Viktoria's life had come, and she felt it so intensely that she felt it all over her body. Her breakthrough at this turning point was Jesus.

'A breaker went before them; they broke the gate and went through and out: Their king went before them, yes, the Lord went before them. Jesaja 52:12'

As we can see from Viktoria's situation, everything changes when Jesus personally intervenes in our lives because He acts in relation to people's needs and because He acts in His divine functions as Creator;

- Creator (John 1:3; Colossians 1:16; Hebrews 1:2)
- Preserver (1 Corinthians 8:6; Colossians 1:17; Hebrews 1:3)
- Author of life (John 1:4; Acts 3:15)
- Ruler (Matthew 28:18; Romans 14:9; Revelation 1:5)
- He heals the sick (Mark 1:32-34; Acts 10:38)
- He teaches with authority (Mark 1:21-22)
- He forgives sins (Mark 2:1-12; Luke 24:47; Acts 5:31; Colossians 3:13)
- He gives healing and eternal life (Acts 4:12; Romans 10:12-13)
- He sends the Holy Spirit (Matthew 3:11; Acts 2:17, 33)

- He raises the dead (Luke 7:11-17; John 5:21)
- He is a judge (Matthew 25:31-46; John 5:19-30; Acts 10:42; 1 Corinthians 4:4-5)

From these scriptural testimonies, we can conclude that Jesus and the Father are one. But the list of testimonies in the Bible is much longer.

"Can we call each other now? My name is Robert. If I am not being too indiscreet, I would like to know why you decided to move to Switzerland after only five months here in Southern Germany," Mr Wolf asks over lunch about the notary's appointment.
"That is a long story. Do you know that you or you are really curious? "
"I am not always so curious, but when it comes to you, I would like to know more," he answers convincingly.

With a blush on her face, as she realised that he was actually interested in her as a person, she tried to open up and began to tell her story, trying to keep it to a minimum. Without once interrupting her, he listened intently, as if he could hear music coming from her lips.

"Your story gets under my skin. When you start to walk with Jesus, everything changes; you start to blossom, you are reborn, and you discover a version of yourself that you never knew. Jesus is life," he said.

At these words, the tears came again to Viktoria, for in one short sentence, she described exactly what had happened to her since she had walked with Jesus. Compassionately, he handed her another handkerchief to wipe away the tears.

"This is the second time today that you have given me a handkerchief to dry my tears. You will think me a crybabe," she said, smiling.
"If the Lord has put so much effort into your life, you must be a very special person."

The man seemed to want to touch her heart. It had been a long time since she had felt she could trust someone since her marriage to Ivan had ended. It did not take long for Viktoria to realise that she was experiencing moments in which one wished time would stand still, in which one wished that something would never end, in which one wished that this moment would last forever. And that usually happens when you are in the presence of someone you like, when you can be there for that moment, when you can look them in the eye, when you can talk to them, when you can touch them with your hands when you can hug them when you can caress them when you can kiss them when you can take them into your heart. But she hardly knew the man, and yet it was as if she had known him for ages. Robert felt the same, and they talked for hours until the shop closed.

"When can I see you again?" asked Robert in the car park.
"You still haven't told me about your wife; how come you're divorced?" asked Viktoria suddenly.

"Maybe because you never asked me," he grinned.

"I didn't want to be curious. Will you tell me then?"

"We belonged to two different faiths, and his religion did not suit my way of practising the faith, which led to daily disagreements and, finally, to the breakup."

Viktoria's marriage ended in a war of interests, and Robert's in a war of faith. But what does the Bible say about finding a mate? True wealth on this earth is success in all its aspects, and that includes our love and family life, not just the economic aspect.

According to the Bible, the search for a life partner is an important aspect of human life. In Genesis 2:18, God explains that it is unhealthy for man to be alone, so He creates a suitable companion, Eve. This teaches us that God has created man in such a way that he seeks companionship and a suitable life partner. God can reveal the future husband or wife of a man in various ways. Prayer is a powerful tool for seeking God's guidance. The individual can ask God for clarity and guidance in the search for a mate by praying sincerely and asking for His will. Circumstances can also play an important role. God can create situations and bring people together in unexpected ways. He can use coincidences, chance meetings, or common interests to lead people to their life partners, partners who not only fill a gap but also match their values, beliefs, and goals.

All this makes us realise that love is important at every stage of life and that each of us's abundance, fulfilment, and happiness are closely linked to the presence and quality of love.

Love is important at every stage of life, but we do not always know exactly what love is. We think that love means "being loved," and we strive in various ways to win the love of others: We strive for wealth and success, take care of our appearance in order to be as attractive as possible, make ourselves likeable and interesting, or try to make ourselves useful.

Or we think that the problem of love is to find the right person. We are convinced that once we have found the right person, we will have no more problems and that life will only go downhill, so we run the risk of chasing love all our lives without ever finding it.

Perhaps because we do not know what love is?

"I give you a new commandment, that you love one another as I have loved you, that you also love one another. By this, all men will know that you are my disciples if you have a love for one another. John 13,34"

No one has greater love than Jesus.

How did Jesus give the best example of unselfish love that a human being can give?

Well, Jesus gave an extraordinary example of unselfish love. Selflessness means putting the needs and interests of others before your own. How did Jesus show this love? He himself said: "Greater love has no one than this, to lay down one's life for one's friends" (John 15:13). Jesus willingly laid down his life for us. This was the highest expression of love a man can give.

But how can we recognise Jesus' love?

Scripture describes the love of Jesus Christ in a truly astonishing way. But how should we respond to the love of Jesus? The Bible exhorts us to "know the love of Jesus Christ, which is higher than all knowledge" (Ephesians 3:19). As we have seen, the account of Jesus' life and ministry in the Gospels teaches us much about his love. However, to truly know Jesus' love, it is not enough to learn what the Bible says about him; we must experience it in practice. If we show love as Jesus has shown it by self-sacrificing ourselves for others, responding with compassion to their needs, and forgiving them from the heart, then we can really understand his feelings. In this way, we can experience 'the love of Jesus which surpasses all knowledge.' And let us never forget: the more we become like Christ, the closer we come to the One whom he perfectly imitated: our loving God.

"Tell me, did you really go out with a man? But did you not say that you wanted to wait until your body was as it was before? Do you know what I mean, your aesthetic problems because of the breast cancer?" asked Marko, surprised at his mother's change.

"I was like that before Jesus came into my life. It almost looks as if Robert and I were brought together. You know, I was not looking for a man. If I am honest, this man is not only beautiful on the outside but also in his heart," Viktoria replied.

"How can you bear all this? After years of drought, so much has happened in a few weeks; it is quite touching."

"Yes, you are right; with all the tears of happiness, I and the kitchen roll have almost become one..." said Viktoria, amused.
"Your mood also seems to be in top form again. Glory be to Jesus Christ!"

Viktoria was grateful to have had the opportunity to meet a man like Robert, and although she did not yet know how this relationship would develop, she felt the urge to thank the Lord in prayer.

"Dear Heavenly Father,

Thank you for the gift of this new relationship. We are enthusiastic, but sometimes we feel weak and disoriented. We humbly ask you to be our guide. Guide us on your path, and direct our hearts according to your will.

Help us, Lord, to make decisions based on Your truth and not on our fleeting emotions. Make our characters reflect Your love and mercy for one another. Make us communicate with kindness, listen with understanding and give with ease.
Teach us to love sincerely as Christ loves us.
Amen."

After years of trial, ViKtoria had the precious opportunity to choose to live her faith. She was able to pray for the help of Jesus Christ, who knows how to help us. He has experienced every trial we have ever had to face. He knows how to help each one of us. And He loves us. The purpose of life's difficulties is to see what we will choose. Will we practise faith to keep the commandments He has given us in all the trials we face?

"The view from here is beautiful, isn't it?" asked Robert from the top of the hill, taking her hand in his.

"I cannot remember the last time I saw such a view and felt so good," replied Viktoria.

"I often see similar views, but this is the first time that I feel like this, just by holding a hand..."

Chapter 10   Spirituality for Success

"Do you remember the first time you professed your faith in Jesus Christ as your Lord and Saviour? What difference can you see between the before and the after of that confession? How did Jesus become the turning point in your life?" Robert asked Viktoria as they sat on the top of the hill.

Bathed in the warmth of the sun's rays, enveloped in the colours of the blooming spring meadows and soothed by the soft chirping of the birds, Robert and Viktoria spent another afternoon together.

"Wow, so many and so demanding questions; I fear you will have to make notes to remember the answers," she replied amusedly.

"Has so much happened in your life lately?"

"Oh yes, you would not believe how much... If I start to tell you everything, it will get dark," she replied with a smile.

"What impressed you the most?" he asked curiously.

"The light in the darkness, when I had almost given up, especially when I had lost my dreams and thought that my dreams would destroy my life. But on the contrary, it was the turning away from God that destroyed my life, and I realised this more and more as time went on. To be successful in all areas of your life, you only need one thing: Jesus Christ, because in Him we get the power to fulfil all the tasks that God gives us."

"Now you seem to be on the right track ... you have done everything right, too," he grinned.

"How can you say that I have done everything right? You hardly know me..."

"I can tell from afar that you are a man of business and of a certain spiritual predisposition and connection with God. I own half the town, but few people know that because I lead a normal life and do not fall out of favour. Even the restaurant where you sometimes work is mine; the old sick lady and her daughter have leased it from me."

"Excuse me, but if you were a businessman, you would not have needed me to sell your house," she said, astonished.

"Because I wanted to get to know you and because I could see from a distance of three kilometres that your talent was being wasted on the small tasks in a restaurant. Life is all about making decisions, and I wanted to show you that you can do more than just put food on the table... Did you like it? But now get up and go, for you are made for more!"

This man, who seemed to have fallen from heaven, was not only beautiful on the outside but also seemed to be beautiful on the inside. What role did he play in Viktoria's life? Did he provide her with companionship, seduce her, or help her build her business and regain her confidence?

Well, Viktoria, like many of us, has not always made the right decisions in the past. In dark times, she often doubted herself and her work, which led her to reject self-employment and take time to think about whether it was really right to pursue success and work independently. During this time, she worked odd jobs and waited for a message from within before making the decision to set up a property agency in Switzerland.

When her friend Annika could not understand her decision, she put pressure on her, and the friendship broke down.

How much do the opinions of others influence our lives?
Why does society tell us that success is about power, money and materialism? Yet Robert was proof of a healthy way to experience success. He owned half the city, and he was a man of God who worshipped God, loved Jesus Christ, and passionately preached the Word of God every Sunday and holiday.

When we think about how Robert experienced success, we can conclude that success has as many faces as there are people in the world. It is a subjective concept because each of us has his own idea of success, of what is important in life and how to achieve it. Society tells us that we must work hard, be persistent and even ambitious to achieve it. Success is somehow associated with power, money and materialism. Only a few know that the knowledge of one's own spirit as a leadership factor leads to easy success because spirituality is necessary in business life.

Modern leadership consists of the ability to be and remain innovative, to be a powerful engine in an increasingly complex, stressful and sometimes hostile world, and at the same time to create a positive and stimulating climate for oneself, one's employees, one's family members and in general for the people around us.

To create and maintain this balance, the key element of leadership is the ability to steer one's own inner compass.

Is it also possible to combine business and spirituality in order to get back in touch with oneself?

Our culture inevitably leads us to believe that a man or a woman in business should only concentrate on the business and the work in order to earn money and turnover because this is necessary for us to be able to afford to feed ourselves, to have a house and a car, to go on holiday and, yes, even to indulge in luxury from time to time. To be spiritual, however, means to be in touch with one's own soul, which is free and not subject to any constraints. Although we seek this in many different ways, there is only one thing that can satisfy our hearts: an intimate relationship with Jesus Christ. The consistent care of one's spirituality is indispensable in order to remain calm, centred and grounded, whatever happens in our lives and in our activities. It is an essential part that we must pay attention to if we want to be successful without getting lost, but it can be very difficult to do so when we do not know where to start, when we have prejudices against spirituality, or when we live in a very fast life and have a thousand commitments every day. Cultivating one's spirituality means to have a contented heart. A biblical expression for a contented heart is joy. True joy is to have a truly contented heart.

How often do we believe the lie that something other than Christ can satisfy our hearts, and this lie leads us to neglect Christ? As long as we seek satisfaction elsewhere, we will never be satisfied in Christ. Only when we acknowledge Christ as our only treasure will our hearts be truly satisfied.

We are often convinced that success and spirituality are very different experiences. And this belief keeps us away from success because we believe that success keeps us away from spirituality. In reality, success could be described as the widespread feeling of contentment that comes from being who you are and doing what you feel in your heart.

After Viktoria had lost everything, believing that success was the cause of the collapse of her family and her health, she took a break from everything, just in the darkest time of her life, and realised that she had developed a toxic work culture, that the problem was not a success, but the inappropriate use of success and the loss of the connection to herself, the spiritual connection, the connection to God.

'The Lord himself goes before you. He is with you. He will not leave you; he will not forsake you. Deut 31:8'.
This wonderful verse tells us that God never abandons his children in the hour of the storm when we are beaten and walk with our heads hanging and that our God is not an intrusive God. Even if he knows the cause of the disappointment, he gives us time to feel the depth of the bitterness that has gripped us. The result is a confession that is a refrain of human existence: "We hoped...," "but...." How many sorrows, how many defeats, and how many failures are there in the life of every human being? How many times in our lives have we hoped? How many times have we had the feeling of being one step away from happiness and then falling to the ground in disappointment? But Jesus walks with all these discouraged people who walk with their heads

bowed. By walking with them inconspicuously, he gives them back their hope because there is no suffering without resurrection, as Jesus himself has testified to us. And every time we get up after a fall, or when we try to raise up those who have fallen, we are one with him who got up after being crucified: Jesus Christ.

'When you see no way out, call on me for help! I will deliver you, and you shall praise me. Psalm 50:15'

In spiritual life, it is important not to cling to weaknesses but to begin again and again, overcome one's own misery, and conquer timidity. This is how Viktoria's Christian optimism began, when, having felt the drama of her spiritual weakness, she opened herself to the understanding and wonder that, despite her weakness, God had the courage to love her.

Unfortunately, the radically good man, but bound by sin, leads a double life and a double accounting. As a spectator, he is witness to what he is capable of: he becomes aware of his weakness, and he experiences the power of the "strong" who binds him. But he also experiences an inner vitality when he does not accept his wickedness and cries out to the Saviour so that he, the "stronger," can free him and lead him back to inner peace. Then he is no longer paralysed but transformed and proclaims to others the message that it is possible to be healed, to be a forgiven sinner and to rise to a new life.

St Bernard advised: "Do not forget to come to your senses from time to time," and the German writer Goethe said: "Our greatest glory is not that we have never fallen, but that after each fall we always get up again."

It is hard to forgive yourself when you fall again; it is hard to live with your mistakes, but there are no shortcuts on the road to maturity and awareness. One is a mature person only when he accepts his own mistakes.

There is an innate need in us for what is right, true, and good, and when we deviate from this in our behaviour, we feel a deep uneasiness.

God gives us the freedom to carry evil and suffering within us. But every human initiative is answered with a marvellous divine invention. The Father, full of tenderness and mercy, can turn a fall into a "happy mistake" that shows us the generosity of his forgiveness.

We recover from moral illnesses only gradually. For many people, a "good career" of sin and forgiveness is needed before the jolt of an inner earthquake can "stabilise" them in the merciful bosom of the Merciful Father. But it is worth repeating: What counts is the goodwill, the sincere desire to improve in spite of everything.

The Christian life is a spiritual sport (2 Tim 4:7); it is a life in the discipleship of Jesus (Mt 16:24).

It is never too late to live a good life in peace and inner freedom. Nothing is lost forever, and God is always waiting for us to decide to work with him to make our life a living masterpiece of his grace. Let us also stop worrying about our repeated failures and taking it out on God and ourselves. We only need to plunge into the ocean of divine mercy to feel ourselves, with our poet, as "new plants with new shoots."

"Where are we?" asked Viktoria when Robert stopped in front of a hall.

"I want to show you something," he replied.

When Viktoria entered the room, she was amazed to see a lectern, many chairs and boards with messages and Bible verses. Her gaze was drawn to one verse in particular;

"But the Lord stood by me. He gave me the strength to preach the saving message of Jesus in this place and to have people from all over the world listen to it. He saved me from certain death. 2 Timothy 4:17."

"Is this something like a Christian church?" she asked, perplexed.

"No, there is no worship here."

"Then what is being done here?" she inquired.

"I offer free courses in spirituality and success coaching. This room belongs to me. The people who attend the courses do not have to pay me, but they have to do some social work, like cooking for the homeless. See that window there? They can get their food from there if they stand in line."

Astonished and moved, she approached him to embrace him. Wordlessly, he pulled her into a long embrace.

"Why do you do that?" she asked.

"To help others...? You see, I was not always successful; it was a long road full of obstacles, and I fell several times. The last fall was so bad that I thought I would never get up again. But that fall was the turning point in my life," he says proudly.

"Is that why 2 Timothy 4:17 is so big on the board?"

Robert nodded his head in silence.

This is how Jesus introduced Robert to his ideas of charity and compassion.

In the Gospels, we read that Jesus Christ regularly did good deeds for the poor and needy. (Matthew 14:14-21).

But which work had priority for Him? Once, after spending some time with the needy, Jesus said to his disciples: "Let us go to the neighbouring villages so that I can preach there." Why did Jesus stop helping the sick and needy and start preaching again? He himself explained: "For I came to preach. (Mark 1:38-39; Luke 4:43)." For Jesus, it was important to help the needy, but his main task was to preach about the kingdom of God. Mark 1:14.

"Are you grateful to our Lord Jesus Christ for having helped you to achieve your goals by preaching the word and helping the weak?"

"Yes," he said with determination.

"And I thought that only we women could come up with the idea of combining success and spirituality..."

"Apparently not, the group is almost exclusively attended by men, we have only two women among us. Getting back in touch with yourself and generating sales at the same time is not so far-fetched. Culture often leads us to believe that entrepreneurs or career-minded people should focus solely on their business without giving room to spirituality, but in reality, spirituality and business are not opposites, quite the opposite," he says proudly.

With great curiosity and amazement, Viktoria listened to what Robert had to say because it was the same experience she had had herself, and as she evaluated his words, she realised that success and spirituality have nothing to do with being a man or a woman. Indeed, in recent years, the idea has gained ground that in order to lead companies and people and to meet the challenges of work in the best possible way, you have to come "from the depths." The business world is trying to develop a very different approach, where spirituality becomes an integral part of the company. Spirituality in business certainly does not mean daily meditation or religious rituals but any activity in which people get in touch with their souls in order to achieve their goals. Many people have not yet recognised that business life carries in itself distinctive features of spirituality and do not yet see it as such.

Take leadership, for example: How can one be a leader if one does not possess all the abilities that lead to self-knowledge? "Spirituality changes the way we do business," say many leaders and entrepreneurs who have begun to cultivate this new approach in their professional lives.

In order to be successful in the world of work and to have a clear focus on the goals you want to achieve, it is essential to combine these two concepts, which for many are a contradiction in terms. Once you have a clear idea of who you are and what you can achieve through your own efforts, things suddenly take a different turn and move in the right direction.

To run a successful business, you have to start with yourself, not only to improve your own life but also the lives of the people you meet and work with.

Abundance and prosperity are mentioned again and again in the Bible, and it is up to us to find a way to live them sustainably while maintaining our spiritual connection.

"There will be plenty of grain on the earth. Under the reign of Jesus Christ, there will be prosperity and abundance in the material sense. There will be no shortage of food and no famine."

When we think of the whirlwind of emotions and conflicting feelings that the words success and money evoke in most people, it is almost natural that we feel a kind of love and hatred for success. People who hate success and why they usually fail to achieve it When someone hates someone who is better than them, they want to be that way, but they know that they will never be that way, so they start to criticise, mock and "hate" that person because they hate themselves. We need to learn to praise others who are better than us and to improve ourselves by perhaps learning a little from them instead of criticising them. We must ask Jesus to give us courage and help us understand the divine plan that He has for each one of us because He gives us all the tools to change our lives from the bottom up and to achieve true material and spiritual success.

"Grüzi, we have arrived in Zurich," Luka greeted happily at the other end of the line.

"Great, you even speak the Swiss dialect, I just heard," Viktoria made fun of the pronunciation of the word.
"Well, it sounds strange and is hard for us to understand, but we will get used to it because we like it here so much. Zurich has one of the most beautiful old towns I have ever seen, and there is a

beautiful lake, the water is blue like the sea and not brown or green like in Germany. It is like being on another planet..."

"Then I can hardly wait to move my residence and start a wonderful new life in a completely new country," cried Viktoria euphorically.

"But what about Robert? Are you already in love?" asked Marko curiously.

"Well, it is still a bit early to talk about love, but I really like him as a person and would like to get to know him better..."

Viktoria seems to be experiencing a life-changing encounter with Christ, which touches all areas of her life: her spiritual life, the life of her children, her work and, apparently, her emotional life, because every story begins with an encounter which, even if it happens by chance, is always prepared in some way. Sacred Scripture is also full of such coincidences.

The history of the Gospel is the magnificent testimony of a disciple of Jesus who realises that his life is the work of God, who establishes relationships of love, and the more present he is in the lives of people, the more they are united. It is not by chance that the Evangelist John uses the image of Jesus' garment woven in one piece to illustrate the unity, integrity and compactness of the Christian community. Although it is made up of fragile and imperfect human beings, it is like a net that holds together the flock of those called to faith because they do not act by chance or out of self-interest but because they are guided by the Word of God.

The first step in establishing this relationship is to listen to the witnesses and teachers of life. For the two disciples, the Baptist is a companion who awakens a longing in their hearts and, through his witness, encourages them to make choices that lead them in the direction of hope. The doctrine does not consist of a series of concepts to be learnt but is effective in that it prepares the disciple to make his choices, which always involve giving up something. The Baptist is an example of a teacher in faith because, beyond his teaching and his person, he prepared and made possible the "letting go" in order to meet Jesus and to know him personally.

The relationship deepens to the extent that we move from "listening" to "walking and seeing," that is, to the extent that we make life choices that lead us to know ourselves more and more deeply. Our life story, the Evangelist seems to be saying to us, cannot be separated from our relationship with Jesus, just as the threads of a garment could not be held together if the threads of the chain were not numerous and tight. The Apostle Andrew testifies that following Jesus, direct dialogue with him, and intimacy with him does not mean betraying or denying his past and his origins but appreciating them. The joyful message that he brings to his brother Simon means that faith does not isolate us or confine us to small groups. On the contrary, it urges us to be missionaries in the community in which we live or in the family to which we belong. Faith urges us to live in our environment, communicating our personal encounter with Christ through words and gestures of love.

The goal of every mission is the direct encounter with Jesus, as happened to Simon, which truly transforms life, making it not easier but certainly happier. Simon becomes Peter when he allows himself to be seen; that is when he allows himself to be loved and receives the gaze of Jesus, who does not nail him to the wall in his misery but reveals to him his high vocation: to be a support for his brothers and to strengthen them in their faith through his unconditional love for Jesus. The stone is useless if it remains alone, but it is useful if it becomes alive with the others because it builds the holy temple of God, the Church. Peter must let himself be loved by Jesus, and only then can he truly be the first to take the initiative and exercise in the Church the primacy of charity, which unites the diversity of differences.

But how does God lead us to a decision?

Well, first of all, God leads us to an important decision, which is a YES to Jesus. The first revelation we should have is that Jesus is the Lord and Saviour of the life of every human being on earth. Jesus came to suffer, to die and to rise again in order to give life to all those who accept him in their hearts. Revelation is like a staircase that goes up and up. If you remain in Revelation, you remain in the development of your spiritual life. But if you learn to walk in revelation, you will learn that there are many good things with your name written on them. God has already prepared for us things that we will never know until we have an epiphany of the Holy Spirit; God has already prepared for us things not only for a day, not only for a Sunday, not only for a month, not only for a year but for a long time and for eternity.

Only the encounter with Jesus changes our hearts, only the encounter with Jesus, who "changes everything" when he enters our lives, makes us Christians and makes us passionate proclaimers of the Word of God. For "the only one who can change hearts is the Holy Spirit," who also frees us from the temptation to build up an abstraction of a "Christianity without Christ." For what saves lives, changes hearts and makes people happy is not "the idea of Christ" but Christ himself and the work of his grace.

The transformation of the heart and of life is a great sign of Christ's action in us. The transformation that makes us a "new creature." For what changes everything is not an idea, but the very life, as Paul himself says: 'Whoever is in Christ is a new creature. 2 Corinthians 5:17.'

Jesus helps us to be successful, but what does he say about money?

Well, Jesus knows the importance of money in everyday life, as many of his parables show. The Gospel of John mentions that Jesus and his disciples had a common purse (John 12:6; 13:29), and Luke speaks of the women who followed Jesus and the twelve and "served them with their possessions" (Luke 8:3). Jesus does not despise money. Money in itself is neither good nor bad; it depends on what people do with it.

Is money a necessary evil?
No, it is not! Money is a means given by God for the service of all. To despise money is to despise those who need it to live. To

tolerate money as a necessary evil is to cut off one's spiritual life from the carnal dimension. We must be wary of a false spirituality that tries to incarnate itself in all aspects of human life! We cannot pretend that money does not exist. On the contrary, we must see it as a place to which God calls us to serve our brothers and sisters. To despise money or to worship it is the same thing because, in both cases, we do not put it in the right place, and we neglect our deep vocation to serve God and our brothers and sisters with the means he gives us. In both cases, there is a separation between our spiritual life and our daily life: on the one hand, God, on the other, money in its various contexts (family, society).

True spiritual life must not distract us from our concrete duties. This includes the use of money.

However, Jesus is very strict and clear on the question of wealth. You cannot serve both God and mammon. The latter is an Aramaic word for wealth with a very negative, diabolical connotation: the irreconcilable opposition between God and wealth and the irreconcilable covenant between God and the poor; Jesus himself is this covenant. These two principles imply that God and the poor have made a pact with Jesus against their common enemy, Mammon. This justifies the conclusion that spirituality for Jesus, as for his disciples, is "not a struggle against poverty, but a struggle for the poor."

"How many successes have you counted this week?" asked Robert when Viktoria had sold the first flat for the architect.

"Let me count ... I think it goes faster if I just thank Jesus for my whole life."

"Blessed be God for changing lives," shouted Robert.

Chapter 11   Victory through Jesus

S eek your fortune in the Lord: He will fulfil your every desire. Psalm 37:4.

The Bible says that those who think about what they want will become as green as a tree planted by water.

God said to Solomon: "Ask of me whatever you wish."
And Solomon said to God: "You showed great mercy to my father David and made me king in his place; now, O God, let your words to my father David be fulfilled, for you made me king over a people as numerous as the dust of the earth. So now give me wisdom and knowledge, that I may go out and come in before this people; for who can judge your great people?"
And God said to Solomon; "Because thou hast remembered this, and hast not asked for wealth, nor for goods, nor for honour, nor for the souls of thy enemies, nor for long life, but for wisdom and knowledge to govern my people, over whom I have made thee king; I will give thee wisdom and knowledge; and I will give thee wealth, and goods, and honour, such as there was not among the kings before thee, nor such as there shall be after thee." 2. Chronicles 1:7-12.

When we read these lines from the Scriptures, it is immediately clear to us that God does not call Solomon for any reason but to try together to fulfil his desire, and he gives him much more than he had wished for because God's desires are better for us than our own.

In the competition of life, we can be firm, steadfast and successful because we have the final victory through our Lord Jesus Christ.

What God has done through the birth of Jesus Christ, his sinless life, his death, his resurrection, and his ascension enables us to be victorious in every situation. Look into your heart, recognise your feelings and desires and wish for Jesus Christ in your life, because Jesus is the only way to happiness.

The first encounter with Jesus Christ of Nazareth inevitably touches our desires, and it inevitably touches our wishes if it is a real encounter!

To live victoriously and to claim our sufficiency, we draw on the thoughts of God's Word and walk in them with faith. Our battle is in our minds against the spiritual powers that have already been conquered by Christ. We must only recognise that we are what the Word of God says we are, that we have what the Word of God says we have, and that we will be what the Word of God says we will be.

But in the midst of all this, we are conquerors through him who loved us so much. Romans 8:37'.

To be conquerors, we must have the absolute certainty of God's love, for whatever our circumstances may be, no suffering of the present can separate us from God's love. This alone makes us conquerors.

On almost every page of the Bible, we find people wondering about Jesus: where did he come from, how could he teach with such authority, where did he get his strength, why did he work miracles, why did he seem to go against tradition, why did the authorities reject him? These are questions that were asked then and are still being asked today.

Jesus worked with the power and the Spirit of God in Himself during His earthly life (Luke 4:18-21) and also promised to send the Spirit after His resurrection and glorification in communion with the Father (John 14:16 and others). When the apostles received the Holy Spirit on the day of Pentecost, they recognised that Jesus had fulfilled his promise from heaven, and they experienced his transforming power. The Holy Spirit is the soul of the Church to this day. The Christian message includes the Holy Spirit, the true God and the third person of the Holy Trinity. The Christian message proclaims the true God in the words of Jesus Christ.

Jesus gave content to this symbolic expression by pointing to the presence of God in human history and at the end of this history and to the union of God with man. Jesus proclaims that the kingdom of God has already begun through his presence among men and his liberating action against the power of the devil and the evil one (Mt 12:28).

Let us also ask Jesus to come into our hearts because to follow Christ, to love him and to represent him is joy, victory, love, purity, holiness, courage and a feeling of profound freedom. This is Christ. This is the living Christ. This is being Christ. It means to make the love that Christ is and his suffering, which he endured out of love, fruitful. This is the blossoming of love, the blossoming of life, to which Jesus invites us to meet him here in the New

Jerusalem, to be born again to live in Christ, with Christ and for Christ, to embrace the cross of victory, the cross of gold, the cross of light, the cross that enlightens the world, that conquers darkness and gives peace, joy and love, to embrace the cross of gold and the cross of light, the cross that enlightens the world, that conquers darkness and gives peace, joy and love, that exposes and shatters every lie, so that all may live in the truth, in the one truth that saves, that makes conscious and free, as brothers in brother Jesus, who with the weapons of humility and gentleness, of perseverance and love, has conquered the pride and arrogance of this world, to give life to all, to give life to all, so that all may have life and have it in abundance.

"And have you done anything nice with the money from the property sale?" asked Marko.

"No, I am saving it for what I have wanted for almost thirty years, a farm with lots of land and our own animals," said Viktoria resolutely.
"It's unbelievable how much perseverance you have," Marko marvelled.

"What can the fine and strong divine power do?"

"Maybe Robert would like to help you realise your dream; he seems to be a nice guy. You know, I read somewhere in the Bible that when a Christian woman is looking for a husband, she should look for a man 'after the heart of God' (Acts 13:22)" perhaps Robert is such a man.

"I am glad that you think so positively about Robert. I think he is a rare good man. He seems to have been given the gift of wisdom and knowledge of doctrine, the special ability to explain and testify to the truths of the Word of God," she said proudly.

"If the Lord is rewarding him in this way, he must have lived a sinless life, right?"

"If we say that we are without sin, we are deceiving ourselves, and the truth is not in us. Jesus sometimes challenges us and asks us to do something extraordinary, something that goes beyond the limits of the ordinary...."
"Do you still hear that voice inside you that guides you, even now that you are successful again? I think I have inherited it from you because I am beginning to have similar experiences," Marko said.
"To hear the voice of God is not something you inherit, but something you experience when you take him into your heart. As far as I am concerned, I always hear his voice; I feel his presence in me and in everything I do, even if I am successful, and the more successful I am, the more I want to hear his voice and the more I want him to be with me because he is my success!"

Once we understand what Jesus Christ is doing for us, He becomes the most important person in our lives.
If you have ever experienced a natural disaster, if you have ever been the target of a cruel gossip, if you have ever gone through a life-changing trial, if you have ever argued with a friend, or if you have ever had to defend the law, then you know that you need the

peace of the Lord. The peace of Jesus Christ - the peace that quiets the world's raging storms.

Only faith in him makes us conquer the world.

But what is faith? It is the total surrender of the mind to divine truth.

When God revealed his Son, he said to us: "Listen to him" (Mt 17:5), and Christ himself: "I am the only Son of God, and what I know of the eternal mysteries I reveal to you; my word is infallible, because I am the truth" (Mt 11:27; Jn 14:6). By accepting the testimony of Jesus and giving the assent of reason to each of his words, each of his utterances, we make an act of faith.

But it must be a total faith, extending to everything that Jesus Christ has said and done: We must believe not only in his words but also in the divinity of his mission, in the infinite value of his merits and his perfection. Our faith must embrace the whole Christ. If it is still alive and ardent, it throws Jesus at our feet to fulfil all his will; it draws us close to him, never to leave us again: this is the perfect faith unfolded in hope and love.

Faith and perseverance are the essential mixture that will lead us to success in overcoming the world, as Jesus said;

"Have courage! I have overcome the world. John 16:33".

What did he mean by this bold statement? He meant, among other things: The evil in the world has not made me bitter or driven me to vengeance. I did not let the world mould me after its own image.

This applies to all of us! Do not be models for evil in the world; remain true to your values, for remaining true to your values means remaining true to yourself and to our God.

Who can deny that the world today is full of evil? How do we react to injustice and senseless violence? Does it make us angry or lead us to be resentful? How does the moral decay around us affect us? When we add to these human shortcomings and sinful tendencies, we find ourselves fighting a battle on two fronts: against the evil world outside and against the evil tendencies within us. Can we really hope to emerge victorious from this struggle without God's help? How can we ask for His help? What qualities must we develop in order to have the strength to fight the carnal inclinations? To find the answers, let us look at what Jesus taught his beloved disciples on the last day of his earthly life.

Jesus teaches the truth!

Once, after a large number of people had decided not to follow him, Jesus asked the twelve apostles: "Do you not also want to go away?" Peter replied: "Lord, to whom shall we go? You have the words of eternal life" (John 6:67-68).

"Tell me, how many years have you been a successful entrepreneur?" asked Viktoria Robert as she waited for the course participants to arrive.

"Well, I was born with an entrepreneurial streak, but actually, I only became an entrepreneur in the last ten years."

"You know, ten years is a very short time when you consider what you have achieved. In five years, I have not even built up a quarter of what you have, and in two years, I have lost it again. How do you explain that you have remained stable in spite of the emotional stress caused by the divorce?" asked Viktoria without thinking.

"You told me that in order to be successful, you had cut yourself off from everything, including yourself and especially God, but I never stopped involving Him in everything I did, and in times of crisis, I relied completely on Him. At that time, I had just opened the free coaching and spirituality centre and was sharing God's word with everyone who came. This was very fulfilling for me and took my mind off the problems in my family. Do you know that many of those who attended the course are now successful businessmen?"

"Well, your way of being successful was certainly smarter than mine," she said, laughing at herself.

"If you had not been clever, you would not have recognised the problem in the dark times of your life. Instead, as I understand it, you saw it yourself ... for Jesus is intelligence!"

We have been given the gift of intelligence to read the world, not to rewrite it. When human intelligence is busy rewriting the First Principle instead of reading it, it creates a dark, arrogant, domineering way of thinking. When the human intellect is occupied with rewriting the Mother Rule, according to which everything happens, instead of reading it, it creates a deceptive, greedy way of thinking based on separation and delusion. If human intelligence is occupied with rewriting the ultimate purpose of all movements of life instead of reading it, it creates an idiotic and meaningless way of thinking that corresponds to conceit. Human intelligence is not infinite, but when it is occupied with rewriting the meaning of things instead of reading them, it is capable of producing infinite stupidity. The faith of intelligence always sees in everything the connection with the beginning and the whole, the rule of its movement and the goal to which it aspires.

Faith in intelligence is the highest form of intelligence for man, for there is no wiser and wiser way to live than to immerse oneself in the knowledge that we are all and always connected to the First Principle, that everything and everyone moves according to a precise Mother Rule that organises everything and leads to an infinite goal. Faith in intelligence makes recognising and loving the One possible by recognising and loving the Whole. In the face of the All, man can fully recognize the vision of the Triune Face: Father, Son, Spirit.

The intelligence of faith leads to the vision of the All, even though the fragmentation of the every day One into which the Evil One has thrown us. The intelligence of faith leads to the vision of the One, even through the fragmentation of the every day into which this world has thrown us. In a few luminous words, Jesus showed these two faces of faith and pointed to his power and his light: "Whoever has seen me has seen the Father."

For Jesus, it is natural, clear, simple, and certain: 'whoever has seen me has seen the Father.' For Jesus, it is self-evident that to see is to understand, to experience is to know, and to participate is to understand deeply. For Jesus, it is self-evident; it is simple, direct, and illuminating: Whoever has seen Jesus has seen the Father, whoever has known Jesus has known the Father, and whoever has participated in Jesus has participated in the Father.

The faith of intelligence consists in seeing, experiencing, participating in everything that exists, and recognising without a doubt that everything that exists and happens is connected with the first principle, that it always follows a certain rule and is heading towards an end without end. The faith of intelligence is to see, to know, to understand that there is a reason within which everything happens and moves. The faith of intelligence will never be able, not even in its smallest form, to grasp the dimension of chance or luck in existence, just as it is impossible to grasp the absence of water in an ocean. Culture and scholarship are in no way capable of creating and promoting belief in intelligence in human beings; on the contrary, human culture and scholarship make human beings inexperienced, insecure and confused on their way to believing in intelligence. All forms of human culture aim to describe reality, the meaning they do not understand. It is a form of intellectual abuse characterised by the creation of words, concepts, images, and verbal structures to describe something whose meaning cannot be grasped and understood. This frenetic, desperate, ridiculous intellectual activity, whose sole aim is to gain control over life and things, empties people's intentions, words and deeds because it is foolishly and stubbornly determined to describe the meaning of things, while it has not yet grasped their reason, their principle, their movement and their end.

If you succeed with the intelligence of Jesus, you will have lasting success and become a winner in everything in your life in the name of Jesus Christ.

"Mother, should we feel like losers because we have lost our education? You know that the girls have been terrorising us since we started our training in Switzerland. Has Marko already spoken to you?" asked Luka frustratedly.

"Are your girls really causing trouble? No, your brother has not told me anything about it. But why?"

"Now they say we could have done like everyone else and just looked for another job in Germany or declared ourselves unemployed instead of wanting the extra soup and moving to Switzerland. They do not seem to understand that our boss sent us to Switzerland for economic reasons. Girls these days seem to be so busy getting their nails done, wearing permanent make-up and hair extensions to look like Instagram influencers, they don't really notice anything else around them...."

"The negative impact of social media on young people is a fairly well-known and global problem. The growth of social media platforms has brought many benefits, but risks and challenges must also be considered. One does not know how lucky one can be that this door has opened, and one was offered a job in

Switzerland because it is not so easy to get a job there," explains Viktoria.

"But we know it and feel that this is the right way for us..."

It is God who opens and closes doors.

This is what the Holy One, the Truthful One, who has the key of David, who opens, and no one closes, who closes and no one opens, says: 'I know your works.' Revelation 3:7-8.'

There are crucial moments in our lives when we must be especially sure that we hear God's voice clearly. It is not always easy to distinguish His voice from the thoughts dictated by our emotions. But many know from experience that God can open doors to possibilities that no one can close and that He can also close doors that we cannot open.

Jesus has the keys to the gates of Paradise, and He opens a door for every believing soul that no man or demon can close. It will be a joy to discover that faith in Him is the golden key that opens the eternal doors! There is no other. Only Jesus is the "door." There may be good shepherds in life, but no one is the door, only Christ. Anyone who wants to go to heaven must go through this door. All the blessings that come from the Father go through this door. Let us also go through this door with faith and trust. Do you carry this key in your bosom, or do you rely on a deceptive choice that will disappoint you?

O wonderful soul who has reached this chapter and is still reading this book with joy, I invite you to say this prayer:

"Thank you, Jesus, for you have the key to all doors. You always have a solution! You are the answer to my difficulties, and no one can close the doors you have opened. Today, I choose to trust you in the name of Jesus, Amen."

Jesus Christ of Nazareth is the key that opens the way to true life. This King opens our castles to lead us out of the darkness and the shadow of death. Behind each of our sins, there is despair; behind each of our acts of lovelessness, there is an act of resignation; behind our acts that diminish our dignity, there is a narrowness, an inability to bring out the beautiful reality within us. Opening and closing are also an image of the beginning and end. Everything is created, and everything dies in an infinite number of phases. Opening and closing lead us back to the relationships, the dates of our earthly existence, and our affections. Opening and closing show the beginning and end of something and the quality of our decisions. Closing can be better than opening, and vice versa.

"What kind of person do you think I should become to be a man of God? You know that Marko hears this voice within himself that I cannot yet hear. Does that mean God has chosen him more than me?" asked Luka while Viktoria half-finished packing his things for Switzerland.

"Do you want to grow as a man of God?" asked Viktoria, who was completely overwhelmed by the question.

"Yes, what do I have to do for it?"
"You do not have to do anything special except to fully acknowledge God in your life through Jesus Christ because it is "God who makes you grow! Your character is quite different from a few years ago, but you know you still have a long way to go."

'It does not depend on the one who plants or waters but on God, who makes it grow. 1 Cor 3:7'.

God does not demand that man be perfect, but he helps him to grow. Much has been said and written in recent years about women's spirituality but less about men's vocation and mission. Together with some worrying tendencies in our culture to undermine masculinity under the pretext of overcoming a primitivism of the past or excessive dependence on patriarchal structures - not to mention the lack of a father figure in too many families and the need to look to male models - this means that many young men grow up without effective guidance to help them live their masculine identity.
If men would finally realise how wanted and great they are - and according to whose image they were created - they would find it easier to find themselves through love that gives, love that commits, in the following of God who is love. Then, he would also see how far he has sometimes strayed from this state of election and the greatness of his vocation. If man had truly understood and believed that he was created in God's image and likeness and

loved by his heavenly Father, then he would naturally understand his role as a faithful son, caring father, protector and head of his family. Men who live like God and are holy are most needed today; women and children miss them, and many men do. Whether a man is called to be a father, a husband or a celibate, whether he is called to be a priest in perfect chastity, a monk or a consecrated religious, in any case, if he is truly a man of God, prayer and integrity, he will necessarily be a man "for others."

Jesus said: "The Son of Man is not come to be served, but to serve and to give his life as a ransom for many." Matthew 20:28.

At this point, a man might ask himself: Am I still ready to be His disciple in the face of such a clear, strong, and demanding commandment that Christ Himself addresses us? Am I still ready to embody the virtues of respect and responsibility to which he calls me? Am I ready to set limits for the sake of others? Will I use my strength and zeal to care for, protect and educate those entrusted to my care?

Well, we may know all the teachings of the Bible and all the theological terms, we may be able to translate the Bible from the Greek original and so on, but the principle of Micah 6:8 is the principle that the man of God must follow: Do justice, love mercy and walk humbly with him. And above all, do not forget that even with imperfections, you can be a true man of God.

Chapter 12   A heart's desire

"May I?" whispered Robert, kissing Viktoria on the lips as the wind caressed their faces.

A simple kiss, face to face, eyes closed... Viktoria had not experienced such feelings for a long time. Blushing, she stopped and looked at him while he stroked her face.

"I don't know if I've ever felt this before," he murmured, kissing her again.

"I don't know if we've done the right thing because I'm moving to Switzerland in two weeks," she murmured, kissing him fiercely.

"1 Cor 13:8: Love never ceases. 1 Cor 13:7: It bears all things, believes all things, hopes all things, endures all things," he replied.

When the gaze of a man who has suffered meets the gaze of a woman who has suffered and is still suffering, the sparks fly. This was the case with Viktoria and Robert.

Their love developed by chance, feelings that wanted nothing more than to be experienced, eyes that, when they met, stole time from words, kisses that left no room for breathing, regret, and guilt. Often, we ask ourselves what is right and what is wrong, whether we should fall in love with someone or not, whether we should go in this direction or run away, but in the end, we always and only decide one thing: we follow our heart, because in these moments it is our only despot that thinks it knows which way we should go, it alone decides on our feelings and actions.

The development of Viktoria and Robert into a spiritual couple, in which authentic spiritual aspirations prevail, ensures their spiritual development and, at the same time, lays the foundation for a relationship that will remain unchanged both in this world and in the next. Cultivating a loving relationship based on mutual love, glorification and continuity, in which the two lovers primarily express genuine spiritual aspirations, is tantamount to consciously acknowledging the fact that the two lovers are first and foremost human beings endowed with an immortal Supreme Spirit whose primary purpose is to awaken and develop spiritually.

Love is a wonderful gift with which the wisdom of God has abundantly blessed all who are willing to receive it, for "God is love" (1 John 4:8 and 16).

We find this statement explicitly in the First Letter of the Apostle John, twice within a few verses of each other, but also in the rest of the Bible and the New Testament; this characteristic of God is no less clear.

 "But how could it happen that we should fall in love when I am moving to Switzerland? I hope I am not heading for another catastrophe now that the Lord has helped me to put my life in order," ViKtoria asked, looking to the future.

"It happened because love cannot be planned; it just happens. In Switzerland, too, we will find a way to reconcile love and professional success because 'Where a man works, there is profit; but where a man is content with words, there is lack. Proverbs 14:23'," he replied, handing her a flyer.

"You are very wise, do you know that?" she asked, holding the leaflet in her hand.
"We get wisdom when we ask God to help us. It says so in the Bible, in 1 Kings 3:9... But don't you want to open the flyer and see what it says?" he suggested.

Curious, Viktoria opened the flyer and looked at it.
"This is an advertisement for a Christian centre in Switzerland, do you want me to go there? Is that why you gave it to me?"

"No, I want you to go there with me," Robert replied with a smile. Overwhelmed by her emotions, Viktoria raised her eyes to heaven and cried out: "My merciful Jesus, what have I done to deserve all this goodness?"
God will give you back the years you have lost. So says Joel 2:25, and this happened in Viktoria's life,

'Because you are precious in my sight, and because I love you, I will give men in your place and nations for your life. Jesaja 43:4'.
Since she accepted Jesus Christ into her life, one blessing has followed another because faith has a history, the history of Jesus of Nazareth, which can overlap with the many stories of those who have expressed the richness of her humanity in different times.

Hearing and accepting the Gospel by every finite and changeable human being exposes faith itself to an unimaginable variability of development and growth.

The test of our faith is a problem or a difficulty to which we see no answer. It means that we do not see what God is doing. Faith would no longer be necessary if we could see the answer to a certain situation. For example, if I have to pay a bill and know I will get my salary next week, then I do not need to practice faith. That is, I already know how to get the money for the bill. But if I have a bill to pay and I do not get a salary, or if the bill is higher than I can pay, then I see no solution to my situation. Then, my faith is put to the test. I can then trust God to relieve my distress. This is an example of how my faith is tested. We practice our faith when we do not see the solution.

But faith is not just a matter of material needs. On the contrary, the most common tests of faith are those that have to do with our spiritual state.

The trials of our faith are never pleasant, but we can consider them a great joy. The joy comes not from the suffering that the trial can cause but from the knowledge that the trial brings. Trials produce perseverance, and perseverance works in us to make us complete and whole in Christ.

It is very important to understand that we should not rejoice in the trial itself but in what the trial does. The testing of our faith takes place in those situations in which we do not see and feel God's answer and do not perceive His presence. In these moments, God forces us to walk in faith, to strengthen and consolidate our faith, and to create constancy in us.

These trials reveal the true nature of our faith. They are instruments for the purification and strengthening of our faith.

The word "perseverance" is often translated as "patience" and sometimes as "endurance."
It means to remain steadfast in the face of trials. It means not wavering but continuing in the same direction, keeping an upright heart and not sinning.
Perseverance means looking to God even when we cannot see what He is doing; it means walking both when we see the finish line and when we are in the fog and cannot see any further. It means that we have a map that shows us the way. Sometimes, when the air is clear, we can see the mountains in the distance and have our destination in sight. But it is often foggy, and we cannot see the destination. God calls us to always go forward in faith, no matter how dark or hard it is to see the goal.
There is much we can do to use and deepen the gift of faith that we have received through the Holy Spirit because faith comes from listening to the Word of God.

The activation of her heart transformed Viktoria's life, her relationship with God, her relationship with herself and her relationship with her fellow human beings. Jesus went through her ordeal to win back her heart. If our heart does not remain quite closed, if it lights up a little, if it opens itself a little on this path, which is already our path, then Jesus invites us to go with him on this path.

"I am very glad that I had the opportunity to meet you in person," said Robert when he met Viktoria's sons.

"You must be the man who managed to conquer our mother's heart, which cannot have been easy..." Marko said and shook his hand.

"To be honest, it wasn't that easy..." he grinned.

"And how did you win her over then?" Luka asked.

"I invited them to visit the Christian church I go to... Jesus did the rest," Robert said.

"And where are we invited today since you have not yet told us the reason for your visit?

"That is a surprise," replied Viktoria.

In front of the new rooms of the Christian community, Viktoria's children looked at each other, and then Luka said to Robert: "You seem to have a preference for Christian institutions...."

"Exactly, that is why I have found another one...," Robert replied.

"You founded this centre?" asked Marko in astonishment.

"Yes, and today is the inauguration; the reservations for a visit are skyrocketing."

"Then you have won much today...," said Marko.

"The 'reward' of being a Christian is to look like Jesus: There is no greater reward for those who truly follow the Lord. Besides, I have been rewarded enough in my life since I accepted Jesus into my life. Now it is time to give something back by introducing Jesus to as many people as possible because when the Lord gives you the opportunity to have goods, you must make yourself available, that is, be there for others."

"You are very wise; do you know that?" said Luka.

"Someone told me that recently," he said, referring to Viktoria.

In the plainly furnished room, the illuminated writing on the wall stood out: "I am the way and the truth and the life; no one comes to the Father except through me. John 14:6."

Punctually, at 11 am, the soft music began, accompanied by a hymn to Christ. There were not enough seats in the hall, and people were standing. No corner was left free, and everyone was there to hear the word of the Lord.

During the inauguration, Robert was inspired by a passage from the Gospel of Luke, chapter 11, in which Jesus, after praying and teaching his disciples to pray (v. 1-13), calls his listeners to vigilance and spiritual warfare against the powers of darkness (v. 14-26). At the end of the sermon, a woman praises Jesus and blesses the bosom of those who gave birth to him and nourished him (v. 27): "Blessed is the bosom that bore you, and the breast that nourished you." And he says: "Blessed are those who hear the word of God and pass it on (cf. Lk 11:28)."

To listen to the Word of God and pass it on to be successful in life, to give thanks for success, and to help others be successful as well. That was the mission of Robert and Viktoria with their coaching centre. After all, they felt indebted to Jesus for everything they had, and above all, because they did it out of love for Jesus Christ.

The word love appears 196 times in the Bible. According to the philosopher Søren Kierkegaard, the Bible is God's love letter to us.

Jesus' words of love have inspired millions of people over the centuries. They give orientation and hope to face life's challenges and live compassionately with others. Jesus places love at the centre of his mission and Christian teaching and encourages his followers to be generous, supportive and compassionate towards all people. He defines charity as one of the most important commandments and places it on the same level as the love of God. This principle, known as the love commandment (John 13:34), emphasises the importance of selfless and compassionate love for one's fellow human beings.

These three are Faith, hope, and love.

But the greatest of these is love.

(St Paul, First Letter to the Corinthians)."

When we ask ourselves why love is more important than faith, we must understand that love is not the answer to certain situations but the way out, the turning point! It was out of love for us that Jesus died on the cross, the symbol of God's infinite love for us.

"I have to go out for a moment. My mobile is buzzing. It seems urgent," Viktoria whispers to her son Luka while Robert and Marko stand behind the lectern.

When she looks at the list of calls, she notices that the number she has called is from the town where she used to live. The same number has tried to call her six times in a row. It must be an emergency.

Worried, she calls back, but no one answers. But seconds later, just as she is about to enter Robert's and his children's room, she calls the same number again.

"Mrs Moravec?" asks the male voice at the other end of the line.

"Yes, but who am I speaking to?"

"I'm a senior consultant in accident surgery. Your friend Annika asked me to call you; it is very urgent. You must come as soon as possible."

"You frighten me. What happened to Annika?" she asked with a trembling voice.

"Annika is fine, but her daughter Edina is in a coma after a riding accident...," the doctor summarised.

The shock took Viktoria's breath away, and she was unable to comment on the doctor's words.

"Mrs Moravec? It is urgent," the doctor called.

"I'll be on my way immediately, but it may take me a few hours to arrive, as I am in Switzerland at the moment."

Concerned, Viktoria reentered the room, whispered a few hasty words to Luka and hurried to the exit.

"Heavenly Father, in this time of distress and anguish, I turn to you and ask for a cure for Edina and your divine comfort for Annika and her family. As a shepherd watches over his flock, so I ask You to guide Annika and her family with Your rod through this valley of darkness to protect and comfort them," Viktoria prayed on the plane.

Still not knowing what to expect, Viktoria sought the help of Jesus Christ and continued to pray for God's strength to help her friend Annika through this dramatic time.

I can do everything through Christ, who gives me strength and power. Philippians 4:11'.

These words of the apostle Paul give those who worship God the certainty that they have the strength to do His will. Today, people who worship God can find comfort in these words of Paul. God will give them the strength they need to overcome difficulties and do his will. He can do this by using His Holy Spirit (or his active power), other faithful people and His Word, the Bible (Luke 11:13; Acts 14:21.22; Hebrews 4:12).

When she arrived at the hospital, she immediately accompanied the nurse to the intensive care unit where Annika's daughter Edina was.

When Viktoria entered the room, she saw a shocking scene. Edina lay intubated, and Annika and her husband Anton knelt before the bed. Silently, Annika approached the bed and took Edina's hand in hers. Suddenly, Annika stood up with tears in her eyes, pressed a crucifix into her hand, and said: "I beseech you. I beseech you, pray to your God to heal my child, to listen to you."

Viktoria looked at her friend Annika in amazement and said: "God's goodness is not directed to us by name, but to all who believe in Jesus Christ and ask for it in His name."

"What do I have to do for him to help my child?" cried Annika in despair.

"The prayer is only for those who believe in God and want a personal relationship with Him. I know from experience that love can bring sanctity even in the worst human circumstances, and perhaps now is the right time for you to let Jesus into your life and allow Him to work in your pain. Give Him a chance, and if you want, I will support and pray with you."

After a few seconds of silence, Annika turned to Viktoria and asked: "How is it possible to find faith again when one has never believed?"

"The very fact that you called me here and gave me a crucifix means that you know deep down that there is something greater. But knowing is not enough; you must have our Lord Jesus Christ in your heart," said Viktoria.

When Anton heard these words, he went over to Annika and whispered to her: "Please let us try to do what Viktoria says; let us do it together.

Their conversation was interrupted by Edina's equipment, from which sounds came. Terrified, Annika ran into the hallway and started to call for help.

When the nurse arrived, she took one look at the equipment and immediately called the doctor.

"What's wrong?" asked Annika hysterically.

"Let's wait for the doctor," replied the nurse.

After a thorough examination of the equipment, the doctor took his stethoscope and held it to Edina's chest, next to her heart.

"What's wrong, Doctor?" asks Annika desperately.

"Edina's pulse has accelerated; you can see that on this machine, and the other one has detected a slight brain activity."

Annika went to the machines and looked at the drawings without understanding the results. Then she asked, "Does this mean my daughter will be cured?"

"It is still too early to say because the head injuries are severe, and as I said at the beginning, I cannot make an exact statement at the moment. Everything is in God's hands," the doctor said, leaving the room after making a few entries in the patient's file.

After the doctor had left the room, Anton turned to Annika and asked: "Did you hear what the doctor said? That everything is in God's hands, and why should you not believe him if he says that? You know very well how I think, and I come from an evangelical family that taught me to believe in God before I met you, and we started this atheism that is so fashionable with you. Since when has it been fashionable to turn away from God? Do you know what my parents said when I told them that we had become atheists?"

"Exactly, now everything is my fault. You could have stood your ground or said no," Annika shouted.

"Do you hear how you talk? It is difficult to change your mind when you are convinced of something. Even then, my parents said that God's word says that the sin of turning away from Christ is the worst and most disastrous sin."

"This is not the right time to talk about it, but you will be surprised how many famous people follow the Saviour and are not ashamed to speak publicly about it. I am sure you know Denzel Washington, Antonio Banderas, Oscar-winning actor Matthew McConaughey, and famous Irish actor Pierce Brosnan; they are all people who are not ashamed to profess their faith openly. Let us pray together for Edina, come," said Viktoria.

Viktoria walked slowly out into the hallway, exchanged a few words with the nurse and then returned to the room.

"What have you been doing?" asked Annika as the nurse entered the room with a Bible in her hand.

All three of them sat around the bed, Anton holding the crucifix and Viktoria leafing through the Bible.

"He will wipe away all their tears. There will be no more death, sorrow, pain, and crying," Viktoria read from Revelation 21:4.

Annika and Anton burst into tears and took their daughter's hand when they heard these words. Then Annika knelt down in front of the bed and cried: "Jesus, I beseech you with all my heart, come and save our lives, especially that of our little daughter Edina. I need your help; I can do nothing without you. I repent my sins with all my heart. Please forgive me if I have doubted you and despised you...."

After a gentle pat on the shoulder, Viktoria turns to her friend Annika and says: "You can pray too; it was not so hard. I am proud of you."

"I am ashamed that I treated you so badly; please forgive me," Annika said to Viktoria when the sister announced the end of the visiting hours.

Surely, we all know friends, relatives or acquaintances who once walked with Jesus - and then turned away from him!
The number of persecuted Christians around the world has also increased dramatically. We are so preoccupied with the latest beauty trends, clothes, vegan diets, wars in different countries, corruption, global warming, and social media that we cannot look any further. It is as if someone distracts us from the important and essential values. Jesus is right. We must change course to a simpler life, not a poor life, but a life oriented to the important realities. Perhaps even more than about beauty trends and clothes, it is about the fact that life is taking place increasingly online, that one no longer meets and communicates face to face, that one is isolated and distant. Jesus invites us to trust. To be as if we had not yet had our last beauty treatment or as if our dress was not the last cry. And the feeling of being loved, really loved, gives us that certain something, that charm that no beautician or dress can give us. It gives us the serenity to live our lives and to think only of the essentials without stress, and through the love of Jesus, we automatically radiate a different light, the light of life.

"How is the situation?" asked Robert when he arrived at Viktoria's hotel in the middle of the night.

"According to the doctor, the situation is very dramatic. I will stay here for a few days and support Annika and Anton emotionally and in prayer."

"I'll stay with you," Robert said and hugged her.

"But we only have one bed..." she said shyly.

"Then it is time to share it," he replied happily.

In the early morning, Viktoria was awakened by her mobile phone ringing. When she looked at the display, she saw that Annika was calling, and she was afraid that something had happened.

"I know it is very early, but you have to get ready and come to the hospital; the doctor is waiting for us," Annika said excitedly.

"Why, what happened?" asked Viktoria worriedly.

"The nurse came to the room in the night after hearing a knock and found Edina with her fists clenched. Do you remember the little crucifix I gave you yesterday? Well, yesterday I had left it under Edina's pillow."

"I'll be with you in a minute ... then you can tell me everything," replied Viktoria, overjoyed.

In love, Viktoria jumped on Robert's neck and kissed him tenderly on the lips, "make yourself ready; we need reinforcements in prayer," she said then.

When they arrived at the hospital, they found the doctor in the room examining Edina, his hand still clenched in a fist.

"Could it be a coincidence that her hand is clenched?" asked Annika, the doctor.

"On one hand, the muscles are relaxed; on the other, they are tense. There was also increased brain activity between midnight and 1 a.m. Do you see these waves? It could be anything or nothing. Unfortunately, we cannot say more; anything else would be speculation," said the doctor.

"But doctor, how can you tell? If she moves, that means she is waking up. Right?" asked Annika hopefully.

"Not everything has an explanation ... and no, it could just be muscle reflexes," the doctor said, leaving the room.

With all the excitement about Edina, Annika and Anton had not noticed that Viktoria was with them.

"I brought reinforcements. May I introduce my partner, Robert?" Viktoria asked.

"You have a partner?" asked Annika suspiciously.

"Yes. Why, is that bad?" asked Viktoria to bring some humour into the game.

"Is that bad? It borders on a miracle. We would never have thought that you would get involved with a man again...," Annika replied.

Suddenly and without warning, love entered Viktoria's life, and like pieces of a jigsaw puzzle that illuminated the whole picture, everything became clearer day by day... Soon, her life was completely out of kilter. The fact that she had found Annika again in such a dramatic moment was a gift, a chance to show Annika the mistakes of the past.

"Let's pray for Edina together," Robert suggested, picking up the Bible.

"Does he know how to do that?" asked Annika in surprise.
"He is an expert in this field...," Viktoria replied.
"I have been praying almost the whole night. I could not stop since yesterday...," Anton said in a sad voice, wiping away the tears.

But just as they were about to start praying, the machines started beeping again. Edina's eyes widened, and Annika approached her daughter, shaking her and calling loudly: "Edina, wake up, come to us!"

Immediately, the doctor and nurse came into the room and told Annika to get up from the bed, but she struggled and clung to her daughter. The doctor shone a small torch in Edina's eyes and checked the equipment. Then he noticed that her hand, which was not holding the crucifix, was also cramped and immediately called the senior doctor.
Annika cried hysterically into Viktoria's arms as she tried to calm her.

"Did you hear that?" the senior doctor asked his colleague, referring to the movement of Edina's lips.

"I only saw the lip movement, but I did not hear anything because it is too noisy here," the doctor replied.

The doctor turns to Annika and the others and asks for absolute silence.

"Now I have heard it! She mumbled something," the doctor shouted euphorically.

"Yes, she did that again, something about Yescho or something," said the doctor.

"I understood Yehoshua," said the nurse.

Annika put her hands in her hair and sobbed louder and louder at the doctor: "Do something. Do you not see that my daughter is in delirium?"

"Your daughter is coming out of a coma," the doctor said convincingly.

"But how do you know that? Do you not hear that my daughter is saying incomprehensible things?" asked Annika.

"Your daughter mumbled Yeshua several times very clearly; my colleagues and I heard it. Do you at least know what Yeshua means?" the doctor asked.

"God is salvation. That means God is salvation," said Viktoria.

Annika looked at her daughter, then at the doctor, then at Viktoria, before she lost consciousness and sank to the floor.

Do you believe that Jesus is your saviour? Do you believe that by his death, he has paid in full the debt that your sins have created? Do you believe that his resurrection is the guarantee for your resurrection to eternal life?

Annika has gone from being a chronic atheist to a committed follower of Jesus Christ while going through the worst experience a parent can have. How many of us are able to believe even in the worst and most painful moments of our lives? And how many of us find faith in these moments?

"Well, you baptised?" called Viktoria.

"I baptise you with water, but someone is coming who is stronger than I, and I am not worthy to untie his thong; he will baptise you with the Holy Spirit and fire."
With these words from Matthew 3:11, Robert baptised Annika, Anton and Edina on a beautiful sunny day in the water of a lake on the outskirts of the town where they lived.